William J. Scott

Historic Eras and Paragraphic Pencilings

William J. Scott

Historic Eras and Paragraphic Pencilings

ISBN/EAN: 9783744643290

Printed in Europe, USA, Canada, Australia, Japan

Cover: Foto ©ninafisch / pixelio.de

More available books at **www.hansebooks.com**

Historic Eras

AND

Paragraphic Pencilings.

W. J. SCOTT, D.D.,

NORTH GEORGIA CONFERENCE.

COPYRIGHT SECURED.

Constitution Publishing Co.,
Atlanta, Ga.
1892.

PREFACE.

This volume contains a part only of the literary work of the last two years.

It is gratefully inscribed to friends both new and old —whose steadfast loyalty has been an inspiration to

THE AUTHOR.

January 1st, 1892.

HISTORIC ERAS.

The Story of Magna Charta.

"England is the freest country in the world.—*Montesquieu.*"

It is a singular fact that Henry Hallam, in the main an astute and learned historian, should have commenced his "Constitutional History of England" with the accession of Henry VII. It is as though Von Holst, or whoever else should undertake a constitutional history of the American government, should utterly ignore the administration of Jefferson and the "era of good feeling" under the presidency of Monroe, and begin with the fatuous and fateful administration of Abraham Lincoln. For while it is true that Henry VII., by his victory on Bosworth field and his intermarriage with Elizabeth of York, united in his own person the rival claims of York and Lancaster, yet the Tudor dynasty that he founded was in many respects the most arbitrary known to English history.

Indeed, the formative period of the British Constitution begins with the reign of Henry I., the youngest son of the Conqueror, and culminates in the reign of Edward III., of the house of York. Then it was that Parliament became a two-chambered legislative body, composed of Lords and Commons, the former consisting of the peers, temporal and spiritual, and the latter of the knights of the shire and the burgesses.

If, however, we would rightly understand the story of the *Magna Charta*, we must needs go back to the era of the Norman conquest. That conquest involved the thorough subjugation of the Anglo-Saxon people. They were utterly impoverished by wholesale confiscation. The records of the domesday-book show that in the aggregate not less than six hundred baronies and sixty thousand knightly fees were distributed among the followers of William of Normandy. Besides this impoverishment, there was both political and ecclesiastical disfranchisement. For one hundred years after the decisive battle of Hastings no man of English blood and birth was admitted to the ranks of the nobility. In the Church they were equally discounted by their Norman masters. The prelates and other higher clergy were either born in foreign parts or descendants of those who came over with the Conqueror. The first notable break in this record of Saxon disqualification was made by Henry II. in his nomination of Thomas Becket for the see of Canterbury. The fact that Becket was born on English soil, although of Norman lineage, may have had somewhat to do with his subsequent brutal assassination by a party of Norman gentry.

Beyond all else, however, was the thorough social degredation of the Saxons. Macaulay tells us that during several reigns a Norman could kick an English man with impunity and at will. In a word, they were a despised and downtrodden race.

Henry I., surnamed Beauclerc because of his scholarly attainments, to whom reference has already been made, did much to remedy this social evil and to hasten the ultimate federation of the two races. He earnestly sought to conciliate his English subjects. Some have suggested that he was moved to this by his dread of the rival claims of his eldest brother, Robert, Duke of Normandy, who had grown weary of his crusading adventures. For this purpose it is thought that he espoused Maude, the daughter of Malcolm, king of Scotland, and of Matilda, the sister of Edgar Etheling, who was unquestionably the legal heir of Edward the Confessor.

Whatever the motive, this marriage contributed greatly to the social uplifting of the English people. The Normans resented the alliance as an open insult to their race, and sought, says one historian, to retaliate by nick-naming Henry "Farmer Godric." The English fully realized the significance of the event, and were jubilant when Archbishop Anselm placed the crown on the head of an English princess. "Henceforward," says the same historian (Green), "the blood of Cedric was intimately blended with the blood of Rolfe—the ganger—the first Duke of Normandy."

Another long stride in the same direction was the issuance by Henry of a charter whose principal provisions were the basis of the Great Charter of Runnimede. Other influences operated to lessen the estrangement between Norman and Saxon, but none nor all of these, including the whole administration of Henry II and the rapid growth of the burgher population, was so effectual as when the two races stood shoulder to shoulder with hand linked in hand in the face of a common peril and in the establishment of a common liberty. This last-named event brings us to the era of *Magna Charta.*

John, the seventh king of the Anglo-Norman dynasty, came to the throne at an evil juncture. A cloud of suspicion hung over him because of the murder of his own nephew, Arthur of Brittany, which murder he is thought to have instigated. This promising young prince was greatly endeared to the English people, not only as the rightful heir to the throne through Geoffrey, the oldest son of the late King Richard, but because he bore the name of the great Keltic hero. The last reason was a mere sentiment, but sentiment is not to be lightly esteemed. In this instance at least it led many to regard the coronation of John with pronounced disfavor. But he came to the throne at an evil juncture for other reasons: he had as a contemporary ruler Philip Augustus, the most chivalric sovereign that had occupied the French throne since the days of Charlemagne.

Philip was the Boulanger of that period, and was intent on the solidarity of France. He was not satisfied that Normandy and Anjou and other provinces should continue as appendages to the Norman kingdom in England, and was determined to expel John from the Continent. The new English sovereign was neither the "coward" nor the "trifler" that Macaulay and Hume have both affirmed. Whatever the defects of his character (and these we do not seek to extenuate), he was neither lacking in courage or capacity. It has been justly said that he was the ablest of the Angevin kings, and that the awful lesson of his life is that it was no idle voluptuary, but the friend of Gerald and the student of Pliny "that lost Normandy, became the vassal of the pope, and died in a desperate fight against English liberty."

The English people were greatly dissatisfied with his civil administration, because of exactions under the name of aids, benevolences, and similar unconstitutional levies in which he exceeded even his father, the lion-hearted Richard. Nor could he inspire them with any zeal for his continental wars waged for the recovery or extension of his domains beyond the channel. But above all were they indignant at his slavish surrender of his crown and kingdom to Radulphe, the papal legate, and his solemn oath to hold England as a fief of the Holy See; so that when he was driven from the Continent by the disastrous battle of Beauvais he found neither respect nor sympathy in his island kingdom.

The statement that he was abandoned by the entire English nobility, except five faithful liegemen, is, perhaps, too highly colored, but it is true that in this extremity he was confronted by "a nation in arms."

We have already intimated that the *Magna Charta* was no essential novelty, but was simply an elaboration and broader application of the principles of the charter promulgated by Henry I. This charter was confirmed by Henry II., but in the later reigns of Stephen of

Blois and Richard I. it was overlooked, and gradually faded from public memory. Just as the book of the law was buried for long years in the rubbish of the temple, until its providential discovery during the reign of Hezekiah, so this priceless charter was afterward exhumed from the dust and *debris* of a monastery. Mankind are chiefly indebted for its resurrection to the researches of Stephen Langton, the Archbishop of Canterbury.

In the mediæval period of European history there was no lack of soldier priests and warrior bishops who, whether in broil or battle, oftentimes exhibited a personal daring worthy of the Spartan Leonidas. Langton did not belong to this class of belligerent Churchmen, but to those cardinal statesmen like Wolsey and Richelieu of a later historic period. While Langton had been thrust upon the English Church and people by the arbitrary act of Innocent III., yet from the beginning he manifested his sympathy for the English people and his reverence for the traditions of Anglo-Saxonism.

In an assembly of the barons at St. Paul's, London, he produced the charter of Henry I., and urged them to make it the basis of their contest with King John. They accepted Langton's counsels, and pledged themselves to its faithful observance.

After divers evasions and subterfuges on the part of the king, with the details of which we are not at present concerned, being hard pressed by the popular clamor and yet more by the primate, he decided to summon the barons and their retainers to a personal conference at Runnimede, an island in the Thames, between Staines and Windsor, henceforth to be esteemed the *incunabula gentis nostrae;* or, as Henry Rogers has translated it, "the cradle of the British giant."

Stephen Langton, with the advice and counsel of the barons, had drawn up the charter which was submitted to John in June, 1215, and after a brief discussion, it was signed, sealed, and delivered and ordered to be published throughout the realm. As a guarantee for its execution, the king, for the time being thoroughly humbled, consented to surrender the city and Tower of London to the keeping of the barons. In addition he accepted the over-lordship of twenty-four of their number, who were empowered by the explicit terms of the Great Charter to levy war against John or any of his royal successors who should attempt its revocation, or even its infringement. Against these obviously hard conditions John raved and gnashed his teeth in impotent rage.

It is now in order to examine some of the leading stipulations of "this key-stone of English liberty."

It is worthy of observation that all classes, clergy and laity, all sorts of men, from the greatest baron to the humblest rustic, were provided for in one or another of its articles.

"The freedom of elections" says Hume, "was secured to the clergy, nor were they compelled to wait for a royal *conge d'elire* and subsequent confirmation of their choice. All checks upon appeals to Rome were removed and the fines imposed on the clergy for any offense were to be proportional to their lay estates and not to their ecclesiastical benefices.

Important restrictions were likewise imposed upon the king, touching the so-called aids exacted of his tenants in chief. These were formally abolished, except in three notable instances; the ransoming of the king in the event of his captivity, the knighting of his eldest son, and the marrying of his eldest daughter. Nor was he hereafter permitted to levy reliefs upon wards when they came to their majority, or to exact of widows any portion of their dower in their husbands' estates. They were also restrained in the matter of compulsory marriages, a royal franchise that had been greatly abused to the sore discomfort of the nobility. It was moreover stipulated that the greater barons should be summoned to the Great Council by special writ, and that the lesser barons should be summoned by the sheriff forty days before the holding of its sessions. The levying of all aids, except the three feudal aids already mentioned, was strictly forbidden without the consent of the Great Council first obtained. We note in this the germ of a great principle which is now fundamental to the British Constitution.

As from a grain of mustard seed there springs a great tree in whose branches the fowls of heaven find shelter, so from this germinal principle has sprung that English law which requires that all money bills must originate in the House of Commons, and that a vote of supplies must be preceded by a redress of political grievances. The English race in both hemispheres have from time immemorial been exceedingly jealous of any encroachment on this line. Emerson has forcefully said that the Englishman is no great stickler about mere abstractions, "but if you lay hands on his day's wages, or his cow, or his right of common, or his shop, he will fight to the judgment." So the American colonists, while yet a feeble folk, resented nothing so much as the policy of the mother country in the matter of parliamentary taxation. In this respect they occupied common ground with John Hampden, who went to prison rather than submit to an unconstitutional levy of twenty shillings. Charles I., despite the abuses of the Star Chamber and of the High Commission court, would have died quietly in his bed, and not as a royal culprit on the scaffold, had he not violated this provision of *Magna Charta*. From it came Triennial Parliaments, Annual Mutiny bills, and eventually the overthrow of the rotten borough system of parliamentary representation. Not a single pound sterling can be drawn from the royal exchequer, either for the civil list or the maintenance of the army or navy, without a vote of the Commons.

Another striking feature of the Great Charter was the provision for a fair and regular administration of justice. Hitherto the court of common pleas was ambulatory—following the king's person from place to place to the serious detriment of suitors and witnesses. Hereafter this important tribunal was required to sit at

Westminster, and the judges of assize as well were compelled to make four circuits annually throughout the kingdom. It was likewise stipulated by the king for himself and his successors that justice should in no wise be sold, denied, or delayed—a most valuable safeguard against judicial negligence and corruption.

In behalf of the merchants and even itinerant tradesmen it was agreed that there should be one weight and one measure for the entire realm, and that this class should have liberty to go and come at will, and should be subjected to no unlawful tolls or imposts. In this connection it was further stipulated that the "ancient liberties" and "free customs" of London and other cities, and even of boroughs, should be conserved.

Hume has well said that if the provisions of the *Magna Charta* had ceased with those already named there would have been little reason for popular rejoicing. But the mailed barons, who wrested the charter from John, were fairly considerate of the welfare of the lower classes. Wherefore it was further ordained that "all the privileges and immunities above mentioned granted to the barons against the king should be extended by the barons to their inferior vassals." As an additional security to the masses it was likewise ordained that "the king should grant no writ empowering a baron to levy aid from his vassals, except the three feudal aids." Likewise, in the 24th section, it was provided that in felonies there should be no forfeiture of a villain cart or implements of husbandry, nor should the small tradesman forfeit "all his wares." In all such cases a sufficiency was left the offender to save him from utter impoverishment. But the chief section was that which furnished a guaranty for the personal liberty of the subject. This is numbered the 39th, and is of itself worth all the blood and treasures that has been expended in its maintenance. This famous section is in the words following: "No free man"—*nullus homo liber*—"shall be taken or imprisoned, or disseized, or outlawed, or banished, or anyways injured; nor will we pass upon him nor send upon him except by the legal judgment of his peers or by the law of the land." It is well understood that the constructions of this section have been exceedingly variant. Sir Edward Coke, the renowned jurist, says in his institutes that "this section involves presentment by a grand jury and subsequent conviction by a petit jury." Thus interpreted it strikes a death-blow at all arbitrary arrests, and unlocks every prison door where a victim of tyranny is confined. For hundreds of years there have been frequent and flagrant violators of these provisions. Indeed, it was never adequately enforced until the great Writ of liberty was secured by the *Habeas Corpus* act in the thirty-first year of Charles II.

It is not out of place to say that in the Bill of Rights prefixed to the Constitution of Georgia, that great popular tribune, Robert Toombs, caused to be inserted this clause: "That the writ of *habeas corpus* shall never be superseded." In the body of the Constitution, however, was inserted the usual exception, "unless in times of invasion or insurrection the public safety may require it." In all cases, however, the party having custody of the prisoner must make some return to the magistrate issuing the writ. No greater tribute was ever paid to the majesty of this law, and the sacredness of the writ based on it, than when Andrew Jackson, after refusing for urgent military reasons obedience to it, subsequently paid the fine of one thousand dollars imposed by the civil magistrates without any sort of compulsion. Such conduct was worthy the hero of New Orleans.

But we here resume the thread of the story of the *Magna Charta*. It is evident that King John yielded to the demands of the barons because there was, for the time being, no possibility of successful resistance. He embraced, however, the earliest opportunity to renew the struggle. For a time, with the help of Rome, he proved an overmatch for the barons and their allies.

The English crown was tendered to Lewis, the son of Philip Augustus, and accepted. Upon the arrival of Lewis, the French followers of John deserted him, and after divers military disasters his kingly fortunes were again reduced to the lowest ebb. Feeble and sore broken, he died in a gluttonous debauch, abandoned of God and despised of men.

Upon the king's death, the English patriots made haste to rid themselves of the royal supremacy of Lewis. By a sort of compromise he was induced to withdraw to the continent. Thereupon, Henry, a natural son of John, was crowned in his ninth year, with

William Earl Mareschal as Regent, the earliest example of a regency in British history. The regent was distinguished for his devotion to the Great Charter, and one of the earliest acts of the new reign was its solemn confirmation by king and council. These confirmations were repeated oftentimes in future years. Indeed, so immense was the popularity of the charter that for several centuries the sovereigns of England, when hard beseiged by popular clamor, were wont to pledge themselves in solemn form to its faithful observance. And yet it is but sheer candor to say that its wholesome restrictions were often trampled upon both by king and Parliament. Notwithstanding, it would again and again assert itself, so that after many bloody contests, even down to the "glorious revolution" of 1688, from which epochal event it has been fully recognized as the basis of the British Constitution. Nor does it savor of exaggeration to affirm that it is now thoroughly interwoven with every fibre of the body politic; and we furthermore reverently say that its line has gone out into all the earth and its sound to the ends of the world.

At the British Museum, in London, among other precious relics of an heroic past, there is one that rivets the gaze of every visitor. It is a tattered copy of the *Magna Charta*. This venerable parchment is yellowed by age and shriveled by fire, and from it depends the royal seal of King John. What the Palladium was to the countrymen of Priam is the *Magna Charta* to the compatriots Wolfe, Sidney and Wellington. By the illiterate English masses it may be reverenced as a sort of national fetich, but by the enlightened Britton it is regarded as the symbol and memorial of a gallant struggle that laid broad and deep the foundation of British liberty. Through all the eight hundred years of England's matchless history, it has been the inspiration of her most illustrious leaders, whether in the arena of arms or in the forum of high debate. In the fourteenth century it nerved Henry V. at the gates of Harfleur, when he once more summoned his discomfited troops to the deadly breach, and gave them as their victorious battle-shout

> Now, God for Harry, England, and Saint George!

The imperishable memory of Runnimede steadied the British infantry amid the storm and stress of Waterloo, when, in the crisis of the conflict, the great Napoleon hurled his "Old Guard" like a thousand catapults against their bristling and impregnable squares

At a later day, even within the memory of men now living, it emboldened the immortal six hundred when they rode right into the "jaws of hell" at the dreadful pass of Balaklava.

These same principles inspired England's great Commoner, the elder Pitt, when in the house of Peers he rebuked with the sternness of a Hebrew prophet the ministry of Lord North, and concluded his masterful Philippic by solemnly invoking the genius of the British Constitution. They tingled in the nerves of our own Henry when, standing in the old House of Burgesses, at Williamsburg, he roused a young nation to arms by his eloquent denunciation of the Stamp Act and the Boston Port bill.

Moreover, we take quite too narrow a view of the scope of the *Magna Charta* if we circumscribe its influence by any geographical limitations. Indeed, in some way it has prompted every manful endeavor for religious and political freedom that has signalized the onward march of universal humanity. Not only among English-speaking people, but among all liberty-loving races, even from old Thermopylæ to New Gettysburg, the principles of that Great Charter have been the rallying cry of downtrodden and yet defiant patriotism.

William the Silent planted himself on these primal truths of government when he cut the dykes of the German Ocean, and let loose the avenging sea on his country's invaders and despoilers. So William Tell, the hero of the Forest Cantons, felt their glow all unconscious, it may be, of their mighty meaning, when he bearded "Gessler" at the gateway of Altorf, and when again he shouted in the ear of the Alpine storm, compared with which "the storms of other lands are but summer flaws," the memorable words:

" Blow on, this is the land of liberty !"

Every intelligent reader will have observed in our hurried comment on the leading provisions of the Great Charter that it contains no dreamy philosophism like the "Utopia" of Sir Thomas Moore, or the "Contract Social" of Rousseau. They will have noticed, likewise, that its statements are more terse and exact than the glittering generalities of our own Declaration of Independence. Rather it is a clear and yet concise embodiment of the principles of statesmanship that must ultimately work out the political redemption of mankind. We speak words of truth and soberness when we say that the enthronement of these principles among all nationalities is the necessary prelude to that golden age of which Isaiah prophesied and Virgil sung. Then, and only then will the story of the *Magna Charta* be ended amid the jubilee of humanity—"redeemed, regenerated, and disenthralled by the irresistible spirit of universal emancipation."

Cromwell and His Times.

A LATE, distinguished writer has said that the horologe of time seldom strikes the great eras of human history. In the main these great eras are unheralded whether by portent in earth or sky, and unannounced by prophecy whether human or divine.

Not one of the four greater prophets of ancient Israel foretold the assembling of the States-general of France in October, 1789, nor the summoning of the Long Parliament of England in November, 1640. Yet these are the pivotal events of modern history. The former was the day dawn, or rather the night-dawn of the era of bloodshed, involving terrorism, Napoleonism, and what else relates to that stormy period of European history. The latter was the birth hour of the Cromwellian era, with its Rupert chivalries and its Ironside invincibilities, with its murder of one king and the precipitate flight of another. To this last named historic period we dvote this paper on Cromwell and his times.

In the closing year of the sixteenth century, in the pretty village of Huntingdon, a man-child was born into the world, who five days thereafter in the parish church was christened "Oliver." This happening excited no interest beyond a narrow circle of village dames, and yet its remoter results have deeply impressed the civilization of the nineteenth century. Of the earlier years of Cromwell we obtain only an occasional glimpse. Possibly, as Greene or Carlyle suggests, he was like most English lads, fond of robbing birds' nests and raiding upon apple orchards. We believe it is Dickens who mentions an interview between Cromwell and Charles I., at the house of Sir Oliver Cromwell, the uncle of the future Protector, when they were both mere lads. As the story goes, young Oliver manifested some repugnance to his Royal Highness, and peremptorily refused to "pay his duty" to the forthcoming king. It is spoken to the credit of James I., who was present at the interview, that he commended the sturdy independence of young Cromwell, and reminded his favorite son that the English people all had the same pluck with his boyish playmate. The whole statement is probably mythical, and was the after-thought of some later narrator.

When about the age of seventeen, Cromwell came under the influence of the Puritan clergy, who were wont to harangue the village rabble at the foot of the town cross. In due time he embraced the Puritan theology. This was shortly followed by his conversion, a phenomenal event that might be compared to that of John Bunyan, the tinker of Elstow. About this time he was troubled with those hypochondriac fancies of which Carlyle has preserved the account. Amongst other odd conceits was his sending to the village physician at midnight, fearing that he was about to die. By degrees, however, he emerged from this valley of the shadow of death, so that in his last days he desired neither refreshment nor sleep, but was in haste to be gone.

Whether wisely or not, Cromwell, at an immature age, espoused Elizabeth, the daughter of Sir James Bourchier, who proved a faithful helpmate through all the vicissitudes of an eventful life. For several years after this matrimonial alliance he devoted himself mainly to cattle husbandry, except that at frequent intervals he officiated both in prayer and exhortation in the religious assemblies of his native town. But little else is known of him during this period beyond the fact that he was returned to the Parliament of 1629, where, owing to his "inadequacy of speech," he made no considerable figure. This Parliament was noted for the "petition of right" which Charles I. assented to after many delays and attempted evasions. No sooner, however, was Parliament dissolved than he renewed his unconstitutional levies under the names of loans and benevolences. It is said that upon the dissolution of this Parliament Cromwell remarked in a significant way to his old teacher that they did not need him now, but they would want him hereafter.

During the parliamentary interval of eleven years which followed, Cromwell removed to Cambridgeshire, where he became an expert in all kinds of husbandry. Meanwhile, Strafford had formulated a system of "Thorough," a euphemism for continental despotism. To this period belongs the story that Cromwell, Hampden, Pym, and other commonwealth celebrities secured passage for New England, but were stopped by a royal order in council.

In November, 1640, the Long Parliament, memorable for its political results, met at Westminster in response to the royal summons. In this Parliament Cromwell sat for Cambridgeshire, one of the aristocratic constituencies of the country. At the beginning of this session the House consisted of men of widely different views in politics and religion. Were we to classify according to the French method, we should say there was a center and a right and left wing. The center, which constituted the dominant faction, was composed of Presbyterians and moderate Church-men under the leadership of Falkland, Hyde, and Colepepper. They were supporters of reform, but opposed to all radical changes in the Constitution. The right wing was made up of pronounced Church-men and believers in the divine right of kingly rule. The left wing consisted of Independents, who had little sympathy with monarchy or Episcopacy They were Puritans in their religious faith, and not a few of them Levelers in their political views. This party, of whom Cromwell soon became the acknowledged head, was recruited in a very small degree from men of gentle birth, like Hampden, and some of nobler lineage, like Essex and Vane.

The parliamentary majority addressed itself at once to reformatory measures The Star Chamber and high commission courts, whose procedure was inquisitorial and at utter variance with English tradition and sentiment, were straightway abolished. At the same time the Parliament voted the imprisonment of Laud and the attainder and subsequent execution of Strafford, whose betrayal of popular liberty could not be condoned and whose evil counsel to the King was the cause of the general discontent which pervaded the masses. These extreme measures aroused the resentment of Charles to such a degree that he committed the most fatal blunder of his reign. He demanded the surrender of Hampden, Pym, and Hollis, and upon the refusal of the House to comply with this demand he ventured on another step that precipitated an armed conflict. Followed by a file of soldiers, he suddenly appeared at the door of the House of Commons for the purpose of seizing five obnoxious members of that body. The House for the nonce behaved with a dignity like that of the Roman Senate when the Gauls invaded that venerable forum. Charles, followed by his henchmen, moved up the main aisle to the Speaker's desk, and found to his sore discomfort that the game had flown. Mortified and crestfallen, he retraced his steps amidst cries of "Privilege! Privilege!" This grave, royal indiscretion was as decisive as Cæsar's passage of the Rubicon. Henceforth the ill-starred monarch determined to stake his political fortunes on the issue of a plebiscitum to be rendered not by ballots, but by bullets. Even at that time the seemingly inevitable conflict might have been prevented by a fusion of the Royalists and Presbyterians. But Charles was obstinate and impracticable, and withdrew from his capitol only to return a doomed and defeated sovereign.

At this point we drop the narrative and speak directly to the personal agency of Cromwell in the great affairs of this commonwealth era. The contest now impending was essentially the immemorial fight between plebeian and patrician, which began at Pharsalia and culminated amidst the disasters of Philippi. On the side of the king were found the principal nobility, the great body of the landed gentry, the clergy almost without a single break, and the two great universities, with their influence. On the side of Parliament were arrayed a small minority of the nobility, a very large majority of the yeomanry and of the merchants and shop-keepers of the realm. Cromwell was but little past forty when the struggle began He was without military training, never having set a squadron in the field, and yet was soon to develop into a commander no whit inferior to the greatest captains of ancient or modern times. In the beginning so little were his possibilities appreciated that he was assigned to no higher position than a captain of dragoons. At the same time such men as the Earl of Essex, as great a dotard as Wurmser, who confronted the young Napoleon in the campaign of Italy, were invested with the chief command. It is not strange, therefore, that for the first two years of the war, the parliamentary forces achieved no brilliant success, and were even placed at serious disadvantage in the northern and western portion of the kingdom. No one was more dissatisfied with these results than Cromwell, who attributed them to a lack of inspiration on the part of the troops.

In a conversation with his cousin, John Hampden, that genial and gallant English gentleman, he remarked that Parliament could not hope to succeed until the struggle was based on religion, and until there was greater thoroughness of drill and discipline.

Upon this basis he organized his world-famed regiment of Ironsides, everyone of whom was a freeholder, *or the son of a freeholder.* This regiment afterwards became the model of the whole army. The effects that soon followed this new military departure were known and read of all men. Heretofore Rupert, the dashing cavalier, had been victorious upon almost every field; but at Naseby and Marston Moor Cromwell's Saints clove them down like so many thistles. The motives of Cromwell may not have been altogether patriotic when he suggested a self-denying ordinance that speedily rid the army of many incapable general officers, and gave the control of military affairs to men like himself, such as Monk, Fleetwood, and his own son-in-law, Ireton, all of whom had that desperate courage which characterized so many of the English leaders from the days of Caractacus. This remodeling of the army was the beginning of the downfall of the Royalist cause. It was not long until Charles I. was placed under military supervision in the Island of Ely, Col. Hammond, a kinsman of Cromwell, having charge of the royal prisoner.

It is well understood that at one time pending the conflict of arms there were negotiations between Cromwell and Charles that, if successful, would have saved the king from the scaffold. These negotiations contemplated the making of Cromwell an Earl of Essex, a title which some of his ancestors had worn. Whether the scheme was defeated by Cromwell's dread of the king's treachery or his fear of the Parliament is matter of conjecture. At any rate, the opportunity was lost and the monarchy plunged forward to overthrow, and Charles himself to death, if not disgrace.

The crisis was not long delayed. A Presbyterian majority of the Parliament had through its commissioners secured what was known as the Newport treaty with the king, which they declared a proper basis of settlement.

Cromwell, who was absent from London conducting the siege of Pontefract, being informed of the state of affairs at Westminster, left the siege in the hands of a subaltern, and hurried to the capital. On his arrival he found things in a bad way for his party, and with his accustomed vigor he set about circumventing the parliamentary majority. He was not a man for rose-water remedies when vast interests were at stake. In this emergency he resorted to a plan that was thoroughly revolutionary. He caused the trained bands of London to be discharged from the custody of the king. At day-break next morning, Col. Rich, with his regiment of cavalry, was ranked in the palace yard for the safe-keeping of his Majesty. Col. Pride, with his regiment of infantry, was stationed at Westminster so as to guard every avenue of approach to the House of Commons. Pride had instructions to exclude every member voting with the Presbyterian majority. This he did with such thoroughness that the Parliament was reduced in number to less than one hundred.

By this direct method, more honest at least than Speaker Reed's later method of counting a quorum, he obtained a majority fully intent on the subversion of monarchy. The Parliament at this time consisted of less than one hundred members, seven-eighths of whom were ready for extreme measures. A committee was appointed to prepare a sort of indictment against Charles Stuart, the King of England, setting forth that said Charles was guilty of high crimes and misdemeanors.

With the merest bit of discussion the Parliament ordered a high court of justice to be organized, with Bradshaw as President. This vehement tribunal convened in the hall of William Rufus, the place of the subsequent trial of Warren Hastings, Governor-general of India. In this hall, according to Macaulay, not less than thirty sovereigns were crowned at different periods of English history. The king was arraigned in due form, and challenged the jurisdiction of the court. Bradshaw replied that the court could not allow its authority to be questioned in that way. After this mock trial the decision was announced condemning Charles, the king, to suffer death on the 30th of January, 1640 (O. S.), in front of the palace of White Hall. Cromwell, who had been rarely present during the investigation, was the third to sign the death-warrant of the king. He has been greatly censured for failing to defeat the execution of the king.

In the existing temper of the army and Parliament it is more than questionable whether his own personal intervention could have averted the blow. A majority, however, of the more conservative citizens of the realm remonstrated against a deed which they regarded as a sacrament of blood. The United Provinces of the Netherlands protested against the act, and the French court was equally emphatic in its condemnation of this proposed judicial murder. At the appointed time, however, the 30th of January, 1640, Charles I. was beheaded in the presence of a vast multitude. His royal demeanor in the presence of his enemies was not less dignified than that of Louis XVI. of France, who in the Place de la Revolution toward the close of the next century suffered the like penalty of decapitation. There was a saying amongst the Greeks that the lightning sanctifies what it strikes; so, likewise, death canonizes its least illustrious victim. How much more when it strikes down one in whose veins flowed the blood of the Plantagenets and the Tudors. The reaction in public sentiment shook the realm from Berwick on the Tweed to Land's End.

From that time forward there could be little enduring peace or abiding reconciliation between the contesting parties until the restoration of the Stuarts. Cromwell, who knew better than any man of his generation the perils of the existing crisis, with as brave a heart as when he stood at Worcester and Marston Moor, addressed himself to the task of reconstruction. Events, however, were not ripe for this reconstructive movement, for at this particular juncture Presbyterian Scotland entered the list as the champion of Charles II. As a precautionary measure, they exacted of him an oath to support the solemn League and Covenant, and straightway mobilized an army for the invasion of England. During this struggle, which resulted in the thorough subjugation of Scotland, occurred two notable battles that deserve special consideration. This brings us to the era of the battle of Dunbar, which illustrates better than Naseby or Marston Moor the superior generalship of Cromwell. The scene of the battle was distant only a few miles from Edinburg. Leslie had intrenched his army on the hill of Doon, confronting Cromwell and his troops, who by some misadventure were shut up in a *cul de sac*, from which there seemed no possibility of escape. Leslie, yielding to the solicitations of the lord commissioners who followed him in his campaigns, unexpectedly left his vantage-ground and descended to the foot of the hill. When Cromwell noticed this blunder of his adversary, he is reported to have said to Monk: "See how the Lord of hosts has delivered them into our hands." He resolved upon immediate attack, but was delayed by the non-arrival of Ireton. To be in readiness, however, he began "shagging," as he quaintly styled it, his army toward the left. In the early twilight of the next day, it being the 3d of September according to the calendar, he set the battle in array, having previously spent a half-hour in devotional exercises.

As the sun rose over the blue German ocean he

quoted the Psalmist's expression, "Let the Lord arise, and let his enemies be scattered," and the army, lifting up their voices in praise and invocation to the tune of "Dundee," which they rolled high and strong at the foot of Doon, they went forward to conflict and to signal victory. This battle was alike typical and decisive. It is hardly credible that the English army, consisting of twelve thousand men, should have nearly destroyed the Scotch army of twenty-odd thousand without sustaining a greater loss than two or three hundred killed and wounded. Just twelve months thereafter the Scots rallied at Worcester, where they again encountered an overwhelming defeat. It was from the field at Worcester that Charles II. was fleeing, when, it is said, that he concealed himself in the branches of the Royal Oak while a surly Roundhead rode below droning a Hebrew psalm. The young king, after divers hair-breadth escapes, reached the Continent, where he remained until the Restoration.

These memorable military successes placed Cromwell in a position that he could safely take up that plan of reconstruction which had been delayed by the Scotch flank movement. The Parliament, as already intimated, had degenerated into a mere handful of sniveling fanatics and psalm-singing hypocrits. The whole country was weary of their legislative incubation. Without formal notice, Cromwell, with a file of soldiers, entered the House of Commons and dispersed what has been very appropriately called the "Rump Parliament." Having cleared the House and locked the door, he put

the key in his pocket. In the doing of this he was
backed by an overwhelming sentiment, both in the army
and country. In re-adjusting the machinery of the
government, Cromwell speedily learned that it was one
thing to conduct a military campaign and quite another
to administer the affairs of a great nation. As one step
toward the accomplishment of this purpose, he summoned a new Parliament, in which many of the rotten
boroughs of that period were disfranchised, and some
of the larger cities which had been hitherto denied parliamentary representation were admitted by their representatives to the great council of the realm. In this he
anticipated the great parliamentary reform of 1832, and
some others of later date. With this Parliament he had
serious trouble, and it was dissolved after a brief session.

Cromwell had now reached the most critical juncture
of his public life. Indeed, he had many reasons to fear
a coalition between the Royalists and the disaffected
Levelers of the army for his personal downfall. To
forestall such a movement, he determined as far as
practicable to restore the ancient forms and symbols of
the British Constitution. He resolved to summon
another Parliament and to reconstruct the House of
Peers as a concession to the nobility, and even to the
middle classes, who had become weary of the religious
dogmas and the political methods of Puritanism.
Accordingly, he invited the leading noblemen to seats
in the Upper House, and, still further to strenghten his
position, he created a number of new peers who were

entitled to no such distinction whether on the score of birth or blood. A majority of them were plebeians who were brought to the surface by their military services in the field. The scheme proved abortive, because the old families were unwilling to sit with these parvenues, and the House of Commons itself strongly refused to recognize these butchers and shop-keepers as part of the ancient peerage of the realm. The Commons, however, tempted him by the offer of the kingly title. He toyed for a season with the seductive bait, and then accepted the less odious title of Lord Protector. Henceforth he administered affairs in a way such as no English sovereign had attempted since the reign of that royal Bluebeard, Henry VIII. He organized England into twelve military districts under the control of an equal number of Major-generals, who were directly responsible to himself. In the same despotic spirit he appointed ecclesiastical "triers," who were as intolerant and proscriptive as the High Commission Court under the management of Laud and his minions. It is the veriest nonsense to condone these flagrant wrongs on the ground that these prelatists and papists were political factions rather than religious sects. It is the merest logical make-shift to reply that Cromwell granted special exemptions to the Jews whilst he punished the reading of the liturgy or the saying of a mass with imprisonment and confiscation. His Puritan defenders never weary of telling us of his sturdy championship of Protestantism on the Continent. Milton, his Latin Secretary, in his sonnets, reminds us of how he demanded freedom of worship for the Piedmontise, and Carlyle tells us of how he threatened that the English guns should be heard in the castle of St. Angelo if the Vaudois were molested in their simple worship Let all this and even more be allowed, yet it remains historically true that in the name of liberty he confiscated the property of the Establishment, robbed the clergy of their livings, and without the color of law ejected hundreds of Presbyterians from their parishes. It is safe to assert that in the closing years of the protectorate he was chargeable with grosser infringements on constitutional law than was Charles I., whom he himself rated guilty of high crimes and misdemeanors. Like Disraeli, of the present century, Cromwell sought to atone for the sins and short-comings of his home administration by the brilliancy of his foreign policy. He it was who secured Dunkirk as some compensation for the loss of Calias and by his admirals despoiled Spain of some of her best colonial possessions. As the ally of Lewis XIV, his soldiery were esteemed the best fighting troops of Europe, and everywhere throughout the Continent the name of Cromwell were a terror to those who would oppose the Protestant cause. It is not strange, therefore, that the character and career of Cromwell has been a perplexity to the historian. Hume stigmatizes him as "a canting hypocrit." Forster, in his "Statesmen of the British Commonwealth," alleges that he was "wanting in truth." On the other hand, Macaulay applauds him to the echo, and Carlyle styles him "the most English of Englishmen."

443311

There is a measure of truth in these different characterizations, and the verdict of the ages will be that he was essentially a bundle of inconsistencies, if not downright contradictions. "In every death-chamber there is the fifth act of a tragedy." This generalization is strikingly true of the last hours of the great Lord Protector. For years his health had been failing, especially from the period of his arduous Irish campaign and the death of his favorite daughter, Elizabeth. Some have supposed that mortified vanity had been at work to undermine his originally vigorous constitution. He had cherished the hope that he might be the founder of a kingly dynasty, or else the head of a European Protestant alliance. These lofty aims were largely frustrated.

In the summer of 1658, he was prostrated by an incurable disease. His days, indeed, were numbered. There was in the manner of Cromwell's death more than a semblance of poetic justice. It occurred on the 3d of September, 1658, the anniversary of the Scots' defeat at Dunbar, and also of what he esteemed his "crowning mercy," the decisive battle of Worcester. In front of the royal palace of White Hall, where he lay dying, had been exhibited nine years agone that most tragical pageant, the judicial murder of Charles I., the purest sovereign of the Stuart dynasty. Almost in the midst of his death-agony, a strong wind tempest swept over the sea and shook even the dry land. Weird lightning flashes, followed by crashing thunder peals, added to the terrible sublimity of the scene. This wild war of the elements without symbolized the fiercer conflict which raged in the breast of the Lord Protector. For months and years he had moved about in hourly apprehension of assassination. Now that the end was nigh there was the absence of that imperial repose with which Cæsar confronted the daggers of conspiracy. Nor was there the slightest token of that exhilaration of soul which the great Napoleon felt when, from his dying couch at Longwood, he seemed to watch the heady surges of some new Leipsic or Austerlitz, and with his parting breath shouted with the old time emphasis: "*Tete d' armee!*" On the contrary, the vultures of remorse were preying on his vitals. In this supreme hour of his destiny his single solace was found in the Puritan dogma: "Once in grace always in grace." A few spasmodic contortions of the face, and the once mailed hand was still and stark in death, and the eagle eye that had so often flashed in the forefront of the charging squadrons was quenched in the blackness of darkness forever.

Whatever may be our estimate of Cromwell's statesmanship, there can be no room for disagreement as to the political consequences of his death. Beyond controversy that death was the downfall of Puritanism in all its branches. He was its brain and its muscle, its blood and its bones. True, he had provided with much painstaking for the succession of his son Richard. But between sire and son there was a broader disparity than between Solomon and Rehoboam. Richard, a well-mannered gentleman, was a sovereign of the Merovingian type, ill-adapted to the existing emergency. His resignation was itself compulsory. The interregnum that followed was marked by the disgraceful rivalry of such military pretenders as Lambert and Desborough. Even the Rump Parliament once more resumed its sittings, claiming to be the representative of the nation. So great and so imminent was the national peril that many of the Roundheads themselves were ready for revolt.

At this juncture Gen. Monk, who with strict impartiality had fought for both king and Parliament, became the man of destiny, Guy Warwick of the hour. Supported by a well disciplined army, he at once entered into negotiations with the cavaliers at home and abroad. The restoration of the Stuarts was decreed, and the national welfare demanded that it be done quickly.

Nothing can give us a clearer idea of the irremediable failure of Puritanism than the stirring events of the next few months. When William of Orange landed at Torbay, he was disheartened by the want of enthusiasm, or rather the stolid indifference that marked his reception. Yet he came on the urgent invitation of the Convention of Westminster, to occupy a throne made vacant by abdication.

How strikingly different the ovation of Charles II.! The booming of guns and the blazing of bonfires announced the joy of the nation that they were at last free from a curse and a pestilence—that *sansculottism* in politics and Jack Cadeism in literature were thrice dead—plucked up by the roots and buried. Nor does it weaken our conclusion that this right royal welcome was extended not to a wise and virtuous prince, who had been defrauded of his birthright, but to a debauchee, who afterward converted the palace into a brothel, and basely consented to become a stipendiary of the French crown. For all this licentiousness in private life, for all the cabal and corruption in official station, Puritanism is justly responsible at the bar of history. Such a reaction, ethical and political, was inevitable, nor is it to be wondered at that it transcended all sober limits. The nation had sown the wind, and must needs reap the whirlwind.

For long years there was on every side confusion and bewilderment as when one is suddenly aroused from some terrible dream. Nor did the reaction exhaust itself with the enthronement of William and Mary. There were still outcroppings of party spleen and somewhat disastrous continental wars until the Peace of Ryswick, in September, 1697. From that date forward the English royal succession has never been for a moment interrupted, nor, indeed, at any time seriously menaced, either by foreign levy or domestic treason.

It will be observed that in this statement we take no account of the Scotch rebellions of 1715 and 1745, or the fabulous adventures of Chevalier St. George in the heart of London.

These abortive attempts and mysterious plottings were of less significance than the No Popery riots and Chartist demonstrations of more recent times. From the era of the restored monarchy the British dominion has widened with the processes of the sun until it has reached the proportions of the grandest imperialism of the world's history.

The England of to-day is the workshop of the nations, the *entrepot* of a commerce whose sales whiten every ocean, the seat of a military power whose "morning drum beat" is more than a sentiment or a sensation; and, what is best of all, the head of a Christian civilization that is destined to overspread the whole earth.

JAMESTOWN AND PLYMOUTH ROCK.

The average American statesman has been slow to apprehend, or else strangely reluctant to acknowledge the existence of two widely divergent civilizations on this continent. Our national coat of arms is emblazoned by the legend, *E Pluribus Unum*, but the stupid conceit is flatly contradicted by almost every page of our national history. Never, except in the presence of a common peril, or under the pressure of a common necessity, has there been more than the faintest semblance of national unity. And no sooner was the external pressure withdrawn than the old antagonisms were revived. In the laboratory of the chemist there is a recognized difference between a mechanical mixture as of water and alcohol, and a chemical combination as of an acid with a metallic base. The one is the result of a well-defined law of affinity; the other is the product of physical contact and commingling. This serves to illustrate what we mean when we assert that strict national unity has never been realized in all the years of our past political history.

It was in somewise formulated in the Articles of Confederation adopted to meet the exigencies of the revolutionary period. It was afterwards rendered more compact in the Federal Constitution of 1787, which, as

John Quincy Adams alleged, was "wrung from the necessities of a reluctant people." It is symbolized in the starry ensign of the Republic, but as for a veritable hand and heart union it is utterly unhistorical. Apart from this truth, the party contests of the last hundred years have been a selfish scramble for official spoils, and the late war between the States is stripped of its heroic aspects, and was the naked outcome of savage bloodthirstiness. In the earliest Colonial records, as well as in the latest phases of representative journalism, these conflicting types of Cavalier and Puritan civilization may be readily recognized. They not only survived the seven years' struggle with Great Britain, but they have outlived the modern era of reconstruction. It is a palpable blunder to suppose that the abolition of slavery, still less the enfranchisement of the freedman, has contributed in any degree to the unification of these diverse civilizations. On the contrary, these events, and others of like sort, have widened the gulf of separation. The traditions of a common struggle for independence have been well-nigh obliterated by the later asperities of sectional conflict. Henceforth, Independence Day has as little political significance in democratic America as the anniversary of the Gunpowder Plot in Protestant England. The 4th of July, alike with the 5th of November, has for all practical uses been expunged from the calendar. It is the part of wise statesmanship to accept these facts and to mold the national policy in accordance therewith. The great problem of our government is not to destroy either of the constituent elements of our American civilization, but to coordinate them in such a spirit of concession and compromise that the blessings of civil and religious liberty may be transmitted to all generations.

SKETCH OF CROMWELL AND HIS TIMES.

In the foregoing chapter, we considered, with some fullness of detail, and we trust with judicial fairness, the chequered fortunes of Puritan and Cavalier through more than a century of conflict on English soil. We witnessed the rise and downfall of Puritanism as a political and religious faction. There is probably a measure of truth in what Macaulay suggests, that the same contest has been continued under other party names down to our own times. So that the recent overthrow of the Gladstone ministry has a vital relation to the political controversies of the 17th century. But we are not careful to analyze or elaborate this statement. We prefer to turn away from these old world struggles and to discuss the more interesting conflict of these civilizations in our Western Hemisphere. The planting of the Jamestown colony was the earliest permanent English settlement on the Continent. The spirit of commercial adventure had mainly to do with this enterprise. There is but the merest modicum of truth in the statement of Northern historians that the colony was, in the beginning, composed of decayed gentlemen and bankrupt traders. The leader of the enterprise and the first governor of the colony, Capt. John Smith, was of highly respectable descent, and a scholar and writer of no little distinction. Like many a knightly spirit of that age, he was a soldier of fortune. He greatly distinguished himself in the war against the infidel Turks, who were menacing the Christian civilization of the West. His nautical skill and his administrative ability were invaluable to the infant colony of Virginia, and because of his admirable qualifications for leadership, he was afterwards chosen by the Puritans as the Admiral of New England.

A majority of those who accompanied Smith to Virginia were, like himself, of gentle birth, so that there was from the outset a predominant element of cavalierism in the Jamestown colony. Some years subsequent, the adventurous Mayflower set forth from Delft Haven, in Holland, with its human cargo of one hundred and odd souls, to find a resting place in the new world. They had fled from England to escape the hardships and disabilities imposed on them by the English establishment. For a few years they had sojourned at Leyden, but a nomadic freak impelled them to a fresh adventure. Their objective point was the mouth of the Hudson river. Owing, however, to contrary winds, and possibly to a nautical blunder, they were drifted or driven to a higher latitude. In December, 1620, they disembarked at Plymouth Rock in the face of hostile savages and in the midst of a climate only less inhospitable than the coasts of Labrador. In numbers and equipment they were a feeble colony. The rigorous winter, coupled with the want of physical comforts, occasioned a very great mortality during the first few months of their settlement. Matthew Arnold has, in a recent publication, spoken jeeringly of the ignorance and coarseness of these Pilgrim Fathers. We shall hardly be accused of undue partiality towards them. But we confess to a feeling of admiration for men who were moved to brave the perils of the sea and to confront the privations of the wilderness, not for gain, but godliness. They were, indeed, illiterate and intensely narrow, but they were sincere and courageous. Nor can it be denied that in that meanly-clad and shivering congregation there was lodged the germ of a culture and a civilization which, with all its faults, has, in the person of some of its representative men, shed imperishable lustre on American literature and statesmanship. These earliest immigrants would have inevitably succumbed to climatic conditions and Indian depredations but for occasional reinforcements of men and supplies, both from England and Holland.

Meanwhile, the struggle for existence developed a toughness of physical and intellectual fibre which has been of material service to their descendants. The timely arrival of Endicott at Salem, and the opportune coming of Winthrop at Charlestown, greatly strengthened the colony. In point of wealth and refinement, these later immigrants were vastly superior to their co-religionists of Plymouth. They soon acquired a political ascendency which they have practically maintained until the present hour. These two colonies, Virginia and Massachusetts, were the geographical centers of the two civilizations that have dominated the religion, literature and politics of the nation for the last hundred years. These mother colonies were antipodal, however, in the matter and style of their civilization.

We shall content ourself with barely suggesting these points of difference, thereby avoiding needless detail and amplification. They differed widely in their theology and forms of worship. The Puritans in both hemispheres accepted the Genevan theology with but the slightest admixture of what was styled at a later date Arminianism. With them divine sovereignty, with its corelated dogmas, as inculcated in the writings of St. Augustine, was the corner stone truth of the Christian system. The latter day modifications of Andover and Yale would have found little favor with the Mathers and Edwardses of a former generation. In church polity they were Congregationalists, regarding each body of faithful men and women as a distinct unit in the kingdom of God. As to forms of worship, they affected great simplicity. Their church architecture was rude and unsightly; their psalmody was the doggerel of Sternhold and Hopkins' version of the Psalter, and they were fiercely intolerant of anything that savored of a liturgical service. They incorporated as far as practicable a theocratic element in their civil economy. Warm advocates in theory of universal suffrage, they made church membership a condition of the elective franchise. While they sought in exile freedom to worship God, they were sternly bent on a monopoly of this priceless privilege. Heresy in doctrine or worldliness of deportment was a species of treason against the godly commonwealth that needed to be restrained and punished by the civil magistrate. Not only the ignorant masses, but their educated leaders were superstitious and cruel to a degree scarcely credible. The death penalty even was inflicted in some instances with unsparing severity on witches, Quakers, Catholics and Baptists. It was as though the shadow had gone back on the dial of Ahaz and professedly Christian men had relapsed into the barbarism of the twelfth century. Like their fellow-fanatics, the Roundheads of England, they were ascetics of the worst type. With them life was not only real, but it was sternly serious and even morose. The Sabbath was a fast to be observed with Jewish strictness—a day to be devoted to sermons, and catechisms, and devout meditation. The blue laws of Connecticut reflect the pious sentiment of the times, and while they are in part apocryphal, they certainly embody the traditional convictions of the Puritan fathers.

It need hardly be said that they were in full sympathy with the popular movement in England. They were jubilant at the victories of Cromwell, and shouted *Te Deum* when Charles I. was executed. They were in good favor with the Lord Protector, and greatly bewailed his death. When the day of reckoning and retribution came to the popular leaders of England, they gladly afforded sanctuary to five of the regicides.

In all of these respects the Cavalier colony was the exact opposite. As regards religion, they were devoted adherents of the Church of England. While Massachusetts divided its territory into school townships, Virginia distributed her territory into parishes, and the book of common prayer was ordered to be used in all religious assemblies. Their churches were fashioned after English models, and many of the private residences of the wealthier planters closely resembled the manor houses of the English gentry. Their homes were the centers of a hospitality that became proverbial for its elegance and bountifulness. Nor were they forgetful of literature and the fine arts. Their homes were furnished with libraries and decorated with statuary and paintings imported from Europe. During the Colonial period, and afterwards, many of the elder sons of these rich planters were educated at the best universities of Europe. In politics they were admirers of the British Constitution with its three estates of king, lords and commons. The common law, with its law of primogeniture, and the feudal system of entails, so favorable to the accumulation of large landed estates, was part of its jurisprudence for nearly two centuries. Instead of manhood suffrage they established freehold suffrage.

They were in hearty accord with the Cavaliers during the commonwealth era, and after the overthrow of the monarchy Virginia was the asylum of hundreds of the persecuted Royalists. Two years before the restoration Richard Lee visited Charles II. at Breda, and tendered him the fealty of his Virginia subjects. Indeed, Sir William Berkley, the Governor of the colony, caused Charles II. to be proclaimed king of England, Scotland, Ireland, France and Virginia, when as yet he was a homeless fugitive. These treasonable doings of the

Virginia Cavaliers did not escape the vigilant eye of Cromwell. He deemed it a matter sufficiently grave to warrant him in dispatching a war ship to reduce the rebellious colony. That veteran Cavalier, Sir William Berkley, organized a body of troops to resist the Lord Protector. Fortunately for the interests of all concerned, an honorable settlement was obtained, Virginia securing for herself the right of self-taxation, and also exemption from commercial burdens imposed on some of the other colonies. It is noteworthy that Virginia was the last to succumb to Puritan ascendency, and the first to challenge the military authority of the English government. For the next hundred years the prosperity of Virginia was phenomenal. Her resources were enlarged in all directions. Especially was she benefited by the influx of an educated and enterprising Scotch-Irish population, who settled west of the Blue Ridge. These Valley Virginians were descendants of the men whose obstinate valor at the siege of Londonderry has made their memory immortal. At first there was a bitter rivalry between these Cohees, as they were called, and the Tuckahoes, who inhabited the tide-water district. Commercial intercourse and frequent intermarriage gradually removed their mutual prejudice. During the French and Indian wars and the Revolutionary struggle, they were more thoroughly united, but their political affiliation was never complete. Stonewall Jackson was a fair representative of the Valley Virginians, while Robert E. Lee was "a Cavalier of the Cavaliers."

Massachusetts and Virginia, although differing on

many questions during the Colonial period, were both jealous of either royal or parliamentary encroachments on their chartered rights.

When, therefore, the Tory ministry of George III. inaugurated their scheme of taxation without representation, they were united in opposition to the project. As early as 1765, the Virginia House Burgesses denounced the Stamp Act as unconstitutional and oppressive. At a later period they made common cause with Puritan Massachusetts against the Boston Port bill, and shipped supplies to their famishing compatriots. To Patrick Henry besides, beyond all men, belongs the credit of starting the ball of the revolution. No man, indeed, did more to arouse the colonists to a just sense of the impending danger.

When the military contest began with a chance collision at Lexington, the Colonies soon became solid. As yet, however, there were few that contemplated a permanent separation from the mother country. In the Colonial Congress, Richard Henry Lee, of Virginia, whose Norman blood was indisputable, moved for the appointment of a committee to draft a Declaration of Independence. The motion prevailed, the declaration was prepared by Thomas Jefferson, submitted to Congress and unanimously adopted. It was at the suggestion of Virginia that the Articles of Confederation were adopted. This was a league between sovereign States, and while it was hardly adequate for the purposes of the war, it proved utterly insufficient after the treaty of Versailles. Many of the States failed to pay their quota towards the support of the Confederation. At times it was so nearly bankrupt that its treasury was barely able to purchase stationery and defray the clerk hire. As stated in the outset, external pressure withdrawn, there was shown an utter lack of political affinity. Anarchy, or a group of feeble and independent republics, it seemed, were the dreadful alternatives. Moreover, the commercial regulations of the different States were so variant that they were a source of perpetual discord. At this juncture Virginia proposed a convention of all the States, to be held at Annapolis, Maryland, which should take all these matters relating to commerce under advisement. So little interest was felt in the question that only four States were represented. This convention of delegates asked for an enlargement of their powers, and adjourned to meet at Philadelphia in May, 1787. Over this memorable body George Washington presided. The session was prolonged through wearisome months of debate, and there were times when the most hopeful despaired of any satisfactory result. Luther Martin tells us that there were no less than three parties in the convention whose differences were radical and apparently irreconcilable. The Constitution, as reported to and finally accepted by the thirteen original States, was the result of a series of compromises. When submitted to the several State conventions, it met with fierce opposition. For somewhile North Carolina and Rhode Island withheld their ratification, and so little desire was felt for what the preamble styled "a more perfect union," that the leading

States of Virginia, New York and Massachusetts adopted it by beggarly majorities. Not a few of our most illustrious patriots and statesmen were dissatisfied in a greater or less degree with the work of the convention. Hamilton himself was not without painful misgivings. Patrick Henry did not scruple to stigmatize the Constitution as dangerous to public liberty. Mr. Jefferson, who was absent in Europe during these heated discussions, was known to be ill-affected towards the proposed change. Viewed in the clear light of subsequent history, some of these men seemed to be endowed with the spirit of political prophecy, not less so, indeed, than Edmund Burke when he wrote his "Reflections on the French Revolution."

They seemed to have an open vision of the rivalry between the hostile sections foreboding anarchy. On the other hand no small number feared the gradual usurpation of the reserved rights of the States by the Central government with an alarming tendency towards imperialism. They predicted the rise of a national party that would seek to obtain by artful construction what was wanting in specific grant. Nor did these far-sighted statesmen fail to see the probability, if not moral certainty, of a struggle between individual States and the Federal government, resulting in such deadly strife as for four years drenched the continent with fraternal blood. As more than once already intimated, the Constitution was at last ratified under a sort of constraint, and not without a significant if silent protest. This language will not be adjudged too strong by those who are familiar with the situation of that transition period. There was reluctant acquiescence rather than hearty approval.

Such was the true condition when the Federal government was launched by the inauguration of Washington in 1789. The immense personal influence of the President prevented for the time being any grave party divisions, guaranteed an era of good feeling, and secured confidence in the stability of the new political order. And yet in his first cabinet there were two distinguished men, Jefferson and Hamilton, who were radically dissimilar in their views on nearly all constitutional questions. These differences were indeed so great that Jefferson withdrew from the cabinet after about three years' service as Secretary of State. There were still, notwithstanding, elements of discord in Congress and in the country which crystalized in well-defined party organization before the close of Washington's second term. It was evident from his farewell address that he clearly foresaw some of the dangers, foreign and domestic, that impended over the new government and threatened to strangle the infant Hercules in its cradle. Hence, his emphatic warning against entangling alliances with foreign nations and his admonitory appeals on the evils of sectionalism.

It was a national misfortune that the official mantle of Washington fell on John Adams, the head and front of the Federal party. For while Mr. Adams was a statesman of incorruptible integrity and tried patriotism, he hardly possessed a single qualification for the Presidency. If not the author of the Jay treaty, he was largely responsible for that diplomatic blunder which practically surrendered the freedom of the seas. His "Defense of the American Constitutions," a prosy and ponderous book, satisfied all thinking men that he was the merest plodder in the science of government. Besides all these proofs of incapacity, his deliberate sanction of the Alien and Sedition laws was such a flagrant outrage on the cardinal principles of American liberty, that he was justly relegated to the shades of Quincy. Against these and similar invasions of personal and State rights, Mr. Jefferson, with the concurrence and co-operation of Mr. Madison, prepared and published the Kentucky and Virginia resolutions. These masterly political documents were henceforth the Magna Charta of State sovereignty and the text-book of the Republican party.

The presidential contest of 1800 was fairly won by the Republicans, but the Federalists, thus early in our national history, sought by mere technicalities to defeat the popular will in the overthrow of Jefferson and the substitution of Aaron Burr, who had hardly been thought of in connection with the Presidency. The struggle in the House of Representatives was long and dubious, and the excitement in the country intense and absorbing. It developed not only a spirit of partyism, but a spirit of sectionalism that has marked all our subsequent history. One of the earliest measures of Mr. Jefferson's administration—we refer to the acquisition of Louisiana —was bitterly opposed by New England and its allies chiefly, if not solely, on the ground that it increased the preponderance of the Southern States. There was, however, no anti-slavery outcry. This fanaticism was the invention of a later age. Abolitionism had as yet neither birth nor self-conscious being. This vast addition to our national territory gave us control of the Mississippi, from its head-waters to the Belize, and made it possible for us to become a first-class political and commercial power. Another thing remained to be done to free us from Colonial vassalage. Our commercial independence, as already intimated, had been seriously compromised by British influence and the servility of the Federal party in the negotiation and ratification of the Jay treaty. The embargo and non-intercourse acts were purely defensive measures, and they aroused the fiercest opposition of the Federal party. All through this struggle for commercial independence, Puritan New England and her allies were in open revolt against the Republican administration.

But for these intestine troubles the second British war might have been indefinitely postponed. The Hartford Convention—the refusal of Massachusetts to respond to the call for the militia—the blue-light signals along the North Atlantic coast, were but the continuous and consistent developments of a well-matured conspiracy against the Federal government. Some partisan writers of American history—it would be a flagrant misnomer to style them historians—have spared no pains to conceal or extenuate these traitorous policies and practices of Federalism. But so convincing was the proof that, as early as 1808, this corrupt organization could only muster eight votes in the Senate, and in a little while it ceased to exercise any marked influence in national politics.

Notwithstanding this defection of New England, the patriotism of the country was equal to the emergency. O r gallant little navy vindicated the rights of neutrals, which had been infringed by the Orders in Council and the Berlin and Milan decrees, and which Jay's treaty had tamely yielded up. Our success on land had likewise been most gratifying. Scott's victories on the Canadian border had been exceptionally brilliant, whilst at New Orleans, Jackson, with his Western riflemen, had routed the veterans of the Peninsular war under the leadership of the gallant, but ill-starred Packenham. The treaty of Ghent for the first time placed our national independence on a firm basis, and the honor is due almost exclusively to the skill and gallantry of the Democratic chieftains in field and cabinet.

The period which immediately followed the administration of Madison is usually characterized as the "Era of good feeling." So complete was the overthrow of Federalism that Mr. Monroe was re-elected to a second term without the slightest show of opposition. The defeat of Jackson and the election of the younger Adams, in 1824, was attributed by a vast majority of the people to a corrupt coalition between "the Puritan and the blackleg." It was fiercely rebuked in the next presidential campaign by the triumphant election of Jackson. It was during this season of domestic quietness that Mexico, under the leadership of Santa Anna and Victoria, subverted the Empire of Iturbide—that Simon Boliva achieved the independence of Columbia and Peru, and that Bozzaris and his "Suliote band" paved the way for the re-establishment of Greek nationality. These triumphs of Democracy on both continents aroused the enthusiasm and enlisted the sympathies of all classes in the United States. They furnished occasion also for some of the finest displays of forensic oratory ever listened to in the halls of the American Congress. This picture of Arcadian repose and loveliness was sadly marred by thrusting upon the country the "Negro Problem." That problem is the ghastly skeleton in our national closet. It is the Sphinx riddle of American politics, which no halting Edipus has yet been found to solve.

Our purpose now is to deal with that special issue which, more than all else, contributed to weaken the bond of fellowship between the North and South, and ultimately to divide the country into geographical parties. The minor questions of tariff, banks, etc., were important, but not of necessity vital. They could in no just sense be regarded as sectional, for while it is true that the Northern section of the Union was most clamorous for protection to domestic industries, there was a respectable minority of Southern voters who were afraid of the competition of the pauper labor of Europe. So, likewise, while the commercial centers of the Middle and Eastern States were chiefly anxious for a national currency of uniform value, yet there were many Southern sympathizers who were dissatisfied with the obvious inconveniences of the State banking system. These questions, however, were susceptible of ready adjustment. The nullification movement in South Carolina was quieted by the compromise of 1833, and the bank troubles were allayed by the heroic conduct of General Jackson. These agitations were not only evanescent, but insignificant compared with the anti-slavery agitation that first assumed political prominence in connection with the admission of Missouri in 1820. This negro craze—for so it may be fitly characterized—was small in its beginnings and had a plausible humanitarian basis. It was for many years confined to the Quakers and a few aged spinsters in the vicinity of Boston, who, in the earlier days of the Plymouth colony, would have been burned as witches. The intelligence of New England ever repudiated it as a mischievous fanaticism. But as the little cloud, which Elijah's servant saw rise out of the sea, continued to spread, until it darkened the whole heavens, so this evil leaven of abolitionism waxed more and more until it imperiled the integrity of the Union. Its foremost champion, Garrison, was dragged, with a rope round his neck, through the streets of Boston, amidst the hootings of the small boys and the curses of what Van Holst styles the "gentlemanly rabble" of the city. Gerritt Smith and Wendell Phillips were frequently pelted with stale eggs and howled down by the mob. But, before many years, it became a political factor of vast weight in State and National politics. The North became jealous, not only of Southern prosperity, but of its continued ascendency in the councils of the nation. There was murmuring against the three-fifths slave representation in the House and complaints against the rendition of fugitive slaves. These fanatics won their first victory in the passage of the Missouri Compromise. While it was a measure of pacification, it was a perilous concession to Abolitionism. By it the South was at once overreached and betrayed. Henceforward the North, while clinging to the humanitarian features of anti-slaveryism, became more arrogant and aggressive. Congress was flooded with memorials praying for the abolition of slavery in the District of Columbia and wherever the General government held exclusive jurisdiction. The halls of Congress resounded with bitter denunciations of the slave-holding aristocracy. Inflammatory appeals were made to the sectional prejudices of the North and West. Men, whose forefathers were brutal task-masters and professional slave-hunters on the coasts of Africa, stood up and lectured the Southern people on the iniquity of chattel slavery. Such a policy of course produced estrangement, and years before the era of bleeding Kansas and John Brown's midnight raid, the two civilizations, correspondent to the two sections, were in as deadly feud as Saxon and Celt.

The rise of the National Whig party in 1836 and its triumph in 1840 promised to allay for a season the feverish excitement on this thoroughly sectional issue. That party embodied a large proportion of the virtue and intelligence of both sections, and for a time kept under control the worse elements that had entered into its composition.

Party ties are not easily broken, nor party allegiance readily foresworn. As long as the two great National parties could preserve their organization intact, there was no ground of apprehension for the safety of the Republic. Two events, however, were at hand which added fresh fuel to the flames. The annexation of Texas and the defeat of Mr. Clay for the Presidency greatly exasperated the Northern extremists. The former, followed as it was by the brilliant campaigns of Scott and Taylor, hardly wakened a momentary enthusiasm amongst the masses of New England. The acquisition of an immense territory, rich in agricultural and mineral resources, was viewed with disfavor and trepidation lest it might strengthen the South and restore the lost equilibrium between the contending sections. The election of Taylor and the compromise of 1850 caused, it is true, a temporary lull, yet it proved to be the calm that precedes the terrible cyclone. The decade that immediately followed was a period of incessant agitation. Compromises had been singularly inefficient. Constitutional compacts were not less powerless to stay the whelming torrent of anti-slavery fanaticism. The Bible and the Constitution were alike spurned as in the interest of slave-catchers and men-stealers, and their sacred restraints trampled under the swinish hoofs of a Circean rabble drunk with partisan fury. The Missouri Compromise was very soon repealed. We, as already intimated, have no disposition to defend it. It was a fraud and an injustice to the slave States. Esau's sale of his birthright for a mess of red lentils was a marvelously shrewd business transaction compared with that political folly. And yet its repeal was the opening of Pandora's box. It fanned the flames of sectional controversy. It substituted squatter sovereignty for constitutional safeguards. It was the proximate cause of that border strife which was the bloody prologue of the fearful tragedy that shortly followed. Nor is it allowable for those who would acquaint themselves with the deeper philosophy of the war between the two civilizations to overlook or undervalue the influence of that remarkable book, Uncle Tom's Cabin. The author was liberally endowed with hereditary genius which had been enriched by more than average literary culture. Whilst there was a coloring of truth in many of its statements, it was in the main a frightful caricature of Southern slavery. Comparatively few of its Northern readers were curious to know the exact truth of its intensely dramatic representations. Whether Topsy was a picture from real slave-life or a figment of the fancy was of no personal concern with them; whether Legree was a flesh and blood entity or the coinage of a distempered brain was of the slightest imaginable consequence. It was quite enough that it nourished their hatred to the Nabobs of Virginia and the Carolinas. It might be easily foreseen that a people who were stirred to incendiary violence by the "awful disclosures of Maria Monk" would be thrilled to their finger tips and infuriated to madness by the overdrawn pictures of

Uncle Tom's Cabin. So profound was the impression that even until to-day the worship of New England is divided between Uncle Tom, the saintly hero of Mrs. Stowe, and Brown of Ossawattomie, the martyr of the Quaker poet, Whittier. Add to this the frantic appeals of a hireling priesthood and of a time-serving, if not subsidized press, and it is not strange that, like a "hell-broth," the Puritan blood continued to boil and bubble with ten-fold fury.

The administration of Buchanan was the close of the constitutional period of our national history. For more than sixty years the South had ruled the destinies of the nation in peace and war. To this statement there are hardly any noteworthy exceptions, and it may be profitable to consider the results, State and Federal, of this protracted dynastic sway. The whole nation had prospered in a degree that may well excite our admiration. In the outset, we were limited on the south and west by French and Spanish occupation. The fairest and most productive portions of the continent were under the flag of European nationalities. These barriers to our territorial extension had been removed, not by war, but by wise and well-directed diplomacy. Our commercial independence, without which our disenthrallment from British dominion would have been of little or no worth, had been achieved by the gallantry of our army and navy. Impressment, right of search, and other hindrances to our national commerce, had been forever abolished. The Monroe doctrine had not only been asserted, but practically enforced. Indian hostilities were largely a thing of the past. The greater portion of the partially domesticated tribes had been removed to reservations provided for them in the far West. These ancient denizens of the forest, under the protection and patronage of the government, had abandoned the chase and engaged in agriculture and the mechanic arts. The financial condition of the country was all that could be desired. The debt incurred by three foreign wars and various Indian disturbances had been liquidated. The excise and land tax system had been discontinued, and with honest and economical administration the revenue from the customs was adequate to meet current expenses. The growth of our population had been normal, and this natural increase was supplemented by a vast immigration from the Old World. The benefits of this immigration had inured in a disproportionate measure to the North, principally because that section had almost a monopoly of direct steam communication with the transatlantic States. Our export trade, consisting mainly of the agricultural products of Southern industry, was constantly enlarging. Indeed, in all parts of the Union there were evidences of enterprise and thrift, as shown by the steady increase of taxable values. Manufactures were flourishing, especially the cotton and iron industries of the Eastern and Middle States, which had for many years been stimulated and fostered by protective tariffs. The South enjoyed its full share of this general prosperity. Despite the alleged economical disadvantages of our labor system, the slave States had increased vastly in material wealth with each successive decade. Georgia alone had added three hundred millions of dollars to her capital from 1840 to 1850. Her sister Southern States had nearly kept pace with her, and probably one or more had out-stripped her. Without the aid of fishery bounties or of incidental protection to her industrial pursuits, she, together with South Carolina and Tennessee, had more wealth per capita than the foremost State of New England. In this estimate we of course rate their negro property and its regular increase at market value. Besides, with all their boasted advantages of common schools, there was a smaller percentage of crime and a larger percentage of higher education in the older Southern States than in the land of steady habits and of moral ideas. These statements may startle, but they are amply sustained by the census statistics.

In two respects the South had relatively lost ground. The numerical strength of the free States had grown more rapidly than the slave States. This, as heretofore suggested, was due in some measure to foreign immigration. And the direction of that current was itself influenced chiefly by the character of the Southern climate and its comparative lack of manufactories. Another relative deficiency of the South was in professional authorship. This has been made the occasion of many spiteful flings at Southern literature. These invidious attacks were prompted by sectional jealousy and echoed by a class of Southern men who neither understand what they say nor whereof they affirm. The small number of professional Southern writers admits of ready explanation. The educated young men of the South devoted themselves mainly to the learned professions, and much the larger part to politics and statesmanship. Hence, it was a matter of general remark, that in the halls of Congress, in the diplomatic service, and in all that pertains to statesmanship in its higher and broader signification, men of Southern birth or lineage have borne away the palm of excellence. Our historic names —Washington, Jefferson, Madison, Marshall, Jackson, Clay, Monroe, Crawford, Calhoun, Preston, Randolph, and a number of lesser lights—were either directly or collaterally of Cavalier blood. But it argues strange ignorance to assert that even in literature and science the South has not produced a large number of notably eminent men and women. She may justly point with pride to Legare, whose equal in the highest Hellenistic culture is rarely found in any age—to Bledsoe, whose Theodicy entitles him to rank with Leibnitz in the realm of theological metaphysics—to Maury, who mapped out the currents of the ocean, and by his "Physical Geography of the Sea" lessened by a hundred-fold the perils of navigation—to Audubon, the world famed ornithologist, who was familiar with every bird of North America, from the humming-bird of the tropics to the eagle of the Rockies—to Calhoun, whose work on Government is a master-piece of political science—to Edgar Allen Poe, whom Victor Hugo pronounces the greatest poet of America, and the superior of Hawthorne as a romancist—to the LeContes, unsurpassed in natural science—to a long array of other names, as Simms,

Warfield, Hayne, Timrod, Wilde, Key, Tucker, Kennedy, Wirt, Longstreet, Alston, Lanier, Charlton, Evans, Ticknor, French, Lipscomb, Thornwell, any and all of whom are worthy of fellowship with the best writers who illuminate the pages of Harper and the Atlantic Monthly. As to periodical literature, it may be gravely questioned whether any American publication, monthly or quarterly, ever reached the standard of literary excellence achieved by the Southern Quarterly Review in its palmiest days.

We say these things without meaning to claim for the literature of either section any extraordinary merit. While we can now properly boast of a "few immortal names," yet it will require at least another half century to develop a distinctive American literature that shall rightfully challenge a place beside the old masters of England, Germany and France. When that time arrives, we venture the prediction that the South will lead the North in literature, as it has heretofore surpassed it in statesmanship. At this point we close our summary of events relating to the constitutional period of American history. The whole country was prosperous and contented, except for that sectional issue which had been persistently thrust upon the nation from the date of the Missouri Compromise.

To this Augustan age of the Republic, future generations will recur with unmixed satisfaction. The next quarter of a century was a period of chaos and misrule. But as the reign of Nero, Caligula and Domitian—the tyrants and scourges of mankind—was eventually succeeded by the age of the Antonines, the "Indian summer" of Roman history, so we cherish the hope that, under the present political auspices, brighter days and grander destinies are yet in store for our common country.

HISTORICAL AND BIOGRAPHICAL SKETCHES.

A Notable Christmas.

December 25, 1776.

The darkest period of our revolutionary struggle was in the early winter of 1776.

The American defeat in the battle of Long Island, the British occupation of New York, and the subsequent capitulation of Fort Washington, involving the loss of three thousand of the best troops of the army, constituted a series of military disasters which threatened the immediate extinction of American liberty.

At this critical juncture, Washington conducted that masterly retreat through New Jersey which won for him the title of the American Fabius.

Nor were these military reverses the only alarming feature of the situation.

The credit of the government had reached its lowest ebb, and would have been utterly wrecked but for the private resources of Robert Morris, of Philadelphia. This patriotic millionaire, in connection with a few others, pledged his individual credit for the support of the lately organized government.

Nor must it be overlooked that desertions were an hourly occurrence, and that the term of enlistment of thousands who still stood at their posts was ready to expire.

After the junction of Sullivan's troops with the main army under Washington, the aggregate force numbered barely five thousand.

There were yet other resources for popular discouragement. Six months had elapsed since the continental congress had solemnly declared that the United Colonies "were and of right ought to be free and independent States." And still France, the hereditary enemy of England, and the natural ally of the struggling colonists, refused to recognize the American commissioners at Paris in their diplomatic capacity.

The French government silently winked at the occasional shipment of arms and other munitions of war from Havre and Bordeaux, but beyond this gave no moral or material aid.

There was still another drawback to colonial success at this momentous crisis. Already there existed bitter rivalry between the leading officers of the army. Especially was Washington badgered and maligned and greatly crippled by Gates, Conway and their fellow compatriots.

Well has it been said by a distinguished historian that the whole movement in behalf of independence seemed on the verge of dissolution.

Philadelphia, the seat of government, was itself so imperiled by the threatened advance of Lord Howe from New York, that it was judged expedient to remove the national capitol to Baltimore.

The time was at hand when it was indispensible that something be done to revive the enthusiasm of a dispirited army. Washington decided to strike a decisive blow in some direction and fortunately the opportunity was not lacking.

Cornwallis, after driving the patriot army beyond the Delaware, proceeded to station detachments at various points on the Jersey side of the river. Trenton and Princeton were two of the points selected.

And now the commander-in chief cast aside the shield of Fabius and grasped the sword of Marcellus. He planned a night attack on the Hessian camp at Trenton.

At this place there was quartered fifteen hundred Hessians, under the command of Colonel Rahl. They were mercenary troops, and, like the southern loyalists of the late federal army, they plundered without stint, and oppressed without mercy. Washington, apprised of their extreme fondness for Christmas cheer and jolity, resolved to make the attack on Christmas night and thus surprise them in their cups.

As the veteran Carthagenians who had followed Hannibal across the Alps were debauched by the luxuries of Capua, so Rahl and his hireling soldiery were demoralized by their drunken festivities at Trenton. They did not dream of a surprise, for the Delaware river was swollen out of its banks and was filled with large quantities of floating ice.

But at midnight the American commander-in-chief succeeded in putting a single division of his army on the Jersey shore. The night was stormy and starless, and so rapidly did Washington execute the movement that the enemy's sentries fired not a single gun.

At 4 o'clock in the morning he struck the camp, uproarious with merriment, and Colonel Rahl, stupefied with beer and whiskey, was shot down while attempting to rally his besotted troops. One thousand of them threw down their arms. The remainder, with a squadron of British cavalry, fled in wild disorder.

Having accomplished his present purpose, Washington recrossed the river with his prisoners a little after daybreak, having lost only four men, two killed and two frozen to death.

In a few days he resolved to surprise the stronger forces stationed at Princeton by another brilliant dash.

This he did on January 2d, 1777. He proceeded by a circuitous route, intending to strike the enemy both in front and rear. By a singular mishap, one wing of his army unexpectedly encountered a British brigade. This wing consisted of fresh recruits, who were so roughly handled that they were being driven in confusion from the field. This temporary advantage gave the main body of the British time to rally for a heavier onset.

At almost the same instant General Mercer, one of the bravest and best of the patriot officers, fell mortally wounded in the thickest of the fight.

In this emergency Washington performed one of those deeds of personal valor that reminds one of Marlborough's desperate charges at Blenhiem. He spurred his horse into the very midst of the opposing columns and with voice and gesture reassured his wavering troops and drove the enemy at the point of the bayonet.

The contest was close and indecisive, but the British loss in killed, wounded and prisoners were four times as heavy as the American loss.

After re-establishing his lines Washington retired in good order to Morriston, where he fixed his winter quarters.

These victories at Trenton and Princeton, which first broke the record of continuous defeat, were an inspiration to the Americans, and in equal ratio carried terror to the hearts of their enemies.

So elated was the continental congress by these exploits of the commander-in-chief that they hastened to invest him, if not the title, at least with the powers of dictatorship. They were followed by more substantial results in the recovery of New Jersey, except New Brunswick and Amboy.

Cornwallis, who had thought that the colonies were virtually subjugated, was about sailing for England. But the Trenton and Princeton defeats so alarmed Lord Howe that he recalled Cornwallis to his command

Thus it will readily be seen that Washington's crossing the Delaware on that notable Christmas night was the pivotal event of the colonial struggle. Not that the patriots were not to experience other reverses in the field and hardships not less severe on the march and the bivouac, as at the Valley Forge encampment, but it broke the record of continuous defeat.

In the September following, Burgoyne's well disciplined army, moving with impervious step down the valley of the Hudson, was checked at Stillwater and forced to surrender at Saratoga. Morgan's corps of riflemen and Arnold's dashing cavalry were more than a set-off to the military incompetence of Gates.

From this time the boasted charm of British invincibility was gone, and in February, 1778, the American commissioners at Paris secured a treaty of Alliance, offensive and defensive, with the French government.

That diplomatic feat, the credit of which was largely due to the wisdom of Franklin, assured the ultimate triumph of the American cause.

The seat of active military operations was, in the closing years of the contest, removed to Georgia and the Carolinas Savannah, Augusta, Ninety-six, Camden, King's Mountain and Guildford Court House, were the strategic points where Greene and Cornwallis and their subalterns wrestled for the prize of empire.

In October, 1781, Cornwallis, the old antagonist of Washington in the Jersey's in 1776, for the last time, stood at bay at Yorktown, Virginia. Greene and Morgan had at last outwitted him in the southern campaign, and now he was like a lion caught in the toils of the hunter.

On the land side he was shut in by the allied armies, American and French, commanded by Washington, with the aid of LaFayette and de Rochambeau. On the seaward side he was cut off from escape by the fleet of de Grasse.

After a fruitless effort to extricate himself from this

veritable *cul de sac*, and despairing of help from Sir Henry Clinton, he decided to capitulate.

It is a striking coincidence that Cornwallis and Washington were once more brought face to face as in the New Jersey campaign of 1776.

But their positions were reversed. Washington had the vantage ground, and on the 19th of October, 1781, Cornwallis surrendered his army of seven thousand men to the American commander.

This virtually closed the contest, but it was not until the resignation of Lord North, the English premier, that the treaty of Paris was ratified, and the independence of the thirteen colonies acknowledged. Thus, as had been said, the obstinacy of an insane sovereign, George III., Great Britain lost the brightest jewels in her crown.

Next Friday is the hundred and sixteenth anniversary of the battle of Trenton. While we feast in moderation under our own roof tree let us remember that little army which crossed the Delaware in the face of storm and sleet, and contributed largely to secure blessings of constitutional liberty.

Old Hickory.

The English people were fond of calling Wellington the "Iron Duke." Not more so than Americans were fond of calling Andrew Jackson "Old Hickory." Both these characterizations indicated the toughness of the mental and moral fiber of these distinguished leaders. Wellington stretched his military lines from Torres Vedras to Waterloo, where the curtain fell on the Napoleonic drama. Jackson won an undying fame at New Orleans, which extended until with one hand he throttled the United States Bank, and with the other squelched the nullification movement

General Jackson, after having suffered defeat in the House of Representatives in 1825, came to the Presidency in March, 1829, by a large majority of electoral votes over his predecessor, the younger Adams.

It was my providential lot to be born on the first anniversary of the inauguration of Mr. Adams. It was a very quiet and uneventful administration, distinguished for nothing beyond the visit of LaFayette, the friend of Washington and of the thirteen colonies in their struggle for independence. From Boston to Savannah he was granted an ovation, and when he left our shores he sailed in a national war ship, the Brandywine, named for the battle in which he had first shed his blood for

American liberty. This Arcadian period of our history was, quite naturally, marked by individual and national prosperity. In a sense, it closed the revolutionary era embracing the fiftieth anniversary of the Declaration of Independence, on which occurred the death of the elder Adams and of his yet more illustrious compatriot, Thomas Jefferson—one the author, and the other the principal advocate of that declaration. In some respects this Adams administration closed likewise the era of good feeling, for the Jacksonian era was both eventful and stormy.

Andrew Jackson brought to the Presidency the instinct of government, backed by an immense will-power. My earliest personal recollection of political events was in connection with the tariff agitation, which was the dominant issue of Jackson's first Presidential term. For some reason the village of Salem, in Clark county, was selected as a rallying point for a State right's demonstration in the year 1832.

There was no very large assemblage, but a procession of some hundreds was formed, and moved with intrepid step to the Methodist Church, where a stirring oration was pronounced by William Crosby Dawson, afterwards a United States Senator. From that time forward, the country, from one end to the other, boiled and bubbled like the witches' caldron in Macbeth. The bitterness between the opposing factions was intense— the administration party denouncing the followers of Mr. Calhoun as "nullifiers," intended to be a term of opprobrium, and the latter retaliating by branding the followers of Jackson as "soap-tails," or "submissionists." Charleston, as in the earthquake of 1887, was the center of this political convulsion. At times there was an ominous speck of war on the horizon, and, as a precautionary measure, Jackson sent a man-of-war to Charleston harbor for the enforcement of the collection of the customs duties. General Scott and a military command were likewise awaiting marching orders. Meanwhile force bills and executive proclamations were discussed by the partisan press, and the Virginia and Kentucky resolutions were debated by village politicians throughout the country.

In this crisis occurred the famous sensational debate between Webster and Hayne.

Forty years ago this month I was standing in the east portico of the Capitol at Washington, and incidentally engaged in a conversation with a venerable gentleman who proved to be one of the oldest inhabitants of that city. Amongst some striking memorabilia of long departed administrations he referred in an interesting way to this Webster-Hayne discussion. He spoke of it as a war of giants, which shook the nation from end to end and from side to side. He regarded the disputants as quite evenly matched, and attributed the seeming triumph of Webster not so much to his intellectual superiority or the intrinsic strength of his position as to the overshadowing influence of Jackson. The gallery and the lobby were packed with the partisans of the administration which put Hayne at a serious disadvantage. I inquired of him as to the immediate effect produced by Webster's thrilling peroration, closing with the memorable words, "Liberty and union now and forever, one and inseparable." He said it was overwhelming and was greeted with an outburst of applause. But he questioned if it was more touching than the passage in Hayne's speech in which he portrayed the weird desolation that would follow the victory of Federalism—a desolation so vast and so complete that

"Not a rose in the wilderness would be left on its stalk
To tell where the garden had been."

He further stated that Mr. Calhoun, who occupied the vice-Presidential Chair, appeared during the debate to be as restless as a caged lion or an imprisoned eagle.

From the portico we walked to the Senate chamber, the arena of this gladiatorial combat. It seemed to me marvelously diminutive to have been the theatre of this historical conflict of oratory and statesmanship. But the time was near at hand when compromise, at best a questionable expedient, or armed contention must ensue.

At this juncture Henry Clay, who had secured the adoption of the Missouri Compromise, stepped forward as a peacemaker in the tariff agitation. The essential feature of the compromise was a provision for the gradual reduction of the duties imposed by the tariff of 1828, as amended in 1831 and 1832, until at the expiration of ten years they should be lowered to a revenue standard. After considerable discussion their compromise was accepted by both belligerent parties, and soon after President Jackson's second inauguration he signed the bill, and for a short season he had handshakings and congratulations. Even South Carolina, which Sergeant S. Prentiss had facetiously dubbed the "hotspur of the union," "smoothed her wrinkled front" and ceased her war talk.

It is well enough to note that this Clay compromise furnished Peel and Wellington a pattern for the English settlement of the same vexatious tariff problem in 1846. There was this difference, however, in the outcome of the two compromises: In England the compact was held sacred, and now wherever the union jack kisses the sunlight and the breeze, free trade is the motto of that wonderful empire. The Whig tariff of 1842 was not an execution of the American compact, but a palpable evasion. A slight reaction occurred under the Polk administration in 1846, but during the last two or more decades the policy of coddling our infant industries of a hundred years old has been pressed by the barons of the spindle and the loom until it reached high-water mark in the McKinley tariff, now being vigorously hammered by Governor Campbell in the Buckeye State. We can hardly believe that this policy, which is but a relic of the middle ages, with no doubtful resemblance to the piracy of the Barbary States, can survive the next presidential campaign. Other issues are important, but none of these must be suffered to stand in the way of a square fight on the tariff question.

Another issue of Jackson's administration was the rechartering of the National Bank. It reached a climax during Jackson's second term, and the bank went down under the herculean blows of the old hero. Efforts in and out of Congress were made to intimidate the President. There was even a vague rumor that an organized mob would march on the Capitol, if needful, to secure a renewal of the charter. General Jackson announced that he would give the leaders as short a shrift as when, without legal warrant, he seized and executed Arbuthnot and Anibuster. "By the eternal," his favorite oath, "let them come! With the people at my back, I will hang the traitors on a gallows as high as Haman!" Not only did he veto the new charter, but before the expiration of the old charter he ordered his Secretary of the Treasury to withdraw from the vaults of the bank every dollar of the Government deposits. Mr. Duane, the head of the treasury department, refused to obey the executive order. Without parleying with that cabinet official, he fired him in a twinkling and appointed Roger B. Taney, of Maryland, his successor, who straightway carried out the President's order. The bank and its friends were indignant at this action, which they stigmatized as a flagrant usurpation. An impeachment was talked of, and, indeed, a resolution of censure was placed on its journal by the Senate. The House refused to concur in this resolution, but it remained on record until some years afterwards, when it was expunged on motion of Jackson's old friend, Thomas H. Benton, of Missouri. Having removed the deposits, the next step was to provide for their safe-keeping. For this purpose a number of State banks were selected as government depositories, and were named, by the opposition, pet banks. As a set-off to the contraction that Nicholas Biddle, President of the United States Bank, started in Philadelphia, the President, through the Secretary, instructed these pet banks to discount liberally for their customers. Not otherwise could the financial crash, already impending, be postponed.

As it was, there followed a season of apparent prosperity. The State banks, being stimulated by the Government, granted discounts on flimsy collaterals. Money was abundant and speculation was wild, especially in the public lands. I was about this time an eyewitness of a very significant scene. It was a company of five or six substantial citizens of Harris county mounted on good horses, each armed with a brace of derringers and their saddle wallets pretty well crammed with paper issues. They were setting out for a long journey through North Alabama to northern Mississippi, where they were to enter public lands.

There were hundreds of such scenes occurring throughout the Southern and Middle States. As a consequence the public land sales became enormous and the treasury received but little gold and silver and an immense quantity of State bank issues. This state of affairs led to the issuance of the famous specie circular requiring all payments into the treasury to be made in gold and silver. Wise men realized that the end of this sort of financiering could but be disastrous, and it came with the fury and crushing weight of an avalanche, of which we gave some account in a former article on the Van Buren administration.

There were two striking episodes in Jackson's second term which we must not entirely overlook.

The principal of these was the French spoliations' claim.

From the origin of the Federal Government our revolutionary ally had presumed somewhat on her kindly offices in that affair to treat our Government rather irreverently. The conduct of the French minister, Genet, under the administration of the elder Adams, was so aggressive, not to say insolent, that we were near being involved in a war with the French directory. Washington, who had retired to the shades of Mount Vernon, was again appointed commander-in-chief, but fortunately the directory recalled Genet, and the diplomatic trouble was adjusted.

At a later period, during the Napoleonic wars, frequent depredations were committed on American commerce under color of the Berlin and Milan decrees. These depredations were made the subject matter of complaint by the American Government, and after much negotiation France consented to pay $5,000,000 as an indemnity. Payment, however, was unreasonably delayed, until in 1835 Jackson demanded a settlement under a threat of reprisals on French commerce, and the breaking off of diplomatic relations. Louis Phillippe, the citizen king, understood quite well the sternness of the American President, and in a little while the indemnity was forthcoming. The other episode, of which we shall only make brief mention, was the Indian troubles in Florida and Alabama. After a good deal of suffering and bloodshed, they were brought to a conclusion by the removal of the Creeks and Seminoles to the Indian reservation west of the Mississippi.

It will be seen that the Jacksonian era was a most eventful period, deserving more elaborate treatment. It ended well, however, and indeed not without considerable eclat. The public debt was entirely extinguished, and a surplus of $40,000,000 was lodged in the national treasury.

Jackson may be said to have designated his successor, and then quietly retired to the Hermitage near Nashville, Tennessee, where he died in 1845, beloved and honored and trusted beyond any political leader since the days of Washington, who will ever be "first in the hearts of his countrymen."

Van Buren and His Administration.

Mr. Van Buren, whom his party friends delighted to call the "Sage of Kinderhook," was a native of that ancient Dutch village which has since grown to a city of respectable dimensions. As his name implies, he was a descendant of some of the early settlers who followed up the discovery of Sir Henry Hudson, one of the great navigators of the seventeenth century.

Mr. Van Buren owed his nomination and election to the presidency much less to his own personal following than to the patronage of "the hero of the Hermitage." Through all the stormy and eventful scenes of the Jacksonian era, he had never wavered in his loyalty to that old chieftain. It was, therefore, no matter of surprise that in the presidential contest of 1836 he received every electoral vote except seventy three, which were cast for General Harrison, South Carolina's vote, which went to Mangum, of North Carolina, and the electoral votes of Georgia and Tennessee, which were thrown to Hugh L. White, of Tennessee.

I saw him twice only, once as he peered through the window of a Piedmont stage coach on his Southern journey. It was only a glimpse. I saw him a second time in 1851, in the cabin of a North river steamer, which plied between New York and Albany. I could detect nothing sinister in the expression of his face or in the tone of his voice, to warrant the aspersion of his political enemies that he was an American Talleyrand, or to justify them in dubbing him the "Little Magician." He was, perhaps, as shrewd as the ex-bishop of Autum, but was neither as crafty nor as unprincipled in his political methods.

He was placed at serious disadvantage by the fact that he was the immediate presidential successor of Andrew Jackson, who was the hero of two or more national wars. The naked truth is, that without any personal default his administration fell on evil days and evil tongues. The oft-quoted saying that his presidential term was "a parenthesis in our national history, that might be read in a low tone or omitted altogether without affecting the sense, is a statement more trenchant than it is truthful.

Some one has said with greater charity that Van Buren's administration suffers by comparison with others because it was an "unheroic period." With the exception of Indian hostilities that first developed that superb half-breed Seminole warrior, Osceola, who was shamefully seized under a flag of truce, and now lies in an undistinguished grave outside the walls of Fort Moultrie, and a Quixotic dash on the Dominion of Canada that was speedily squelched by Federal troops, there was nothing of a military character to break the monotony of the times.

That it was a period of unprecedented commercial

disaster is unquestionable. The forty millions of surplus in the treasury towards the close of Jackson's administration was unwisely, and perhaps unwarrantably distributed amongst the States. It stimulated reckless speculation, and in connection with the specie circular, it had sequestered gold and silver and filled the channels of trade with an irredeemable issue of paper currency.

This was the proximate cause of that condition of threatened bankruptcy which confronted the newly inaugurated President and the country at large in the first months of the Van Buren administration.

Hardly was he comfortably seated in the executive chair before he was urged by the merchants of New York and other Eastern cities to rescind the specie circular and to convene Congress in extra session. Mr. Van Buren, besides being a stickler for "honest money," was too thoroughly wedded to the Jacksonian policy of divorcing the Government from the banks to tamper with the former, but he did meet public expectation in part by calling an extra session.

He went a step beyond this, for in September of that year he advised Congress to provide for the issuance of ten millions in treasury notes to alleviate the existing distress. But his favorite financial scheme was the independent treasury, otherwise called the subtreasury. It simply provided for the safe-keeping and disbursement of the public funds at various business centers It certainly never contemplated making the national treasury a "pawnbroker's shop," where 80 per cent. was advanced on cotton, corn or wheat or lesser agricultural products.

Mr. Van Buren's idea was that this subtreasury plan would be a check on the reckless banking and yet more reckless speculation which had already brought the country to the verge of financial ruin. There was, however, very formidable opposition to this policy, and it was not adopted until 1840. Since that period it has been the basis of our national financial system.

We have already referred in general terms to the prostrate condition of our national industries during Mr. Van Buren's presidential term. Let us speak more in detail and more from personal observation.

In the grain-growing districts of the West wheat and corn were rotting in bins and cribs, with scarcely any quotable market value. The surplus grain stuffs were shut out from the English market by the corn laws. Meanwhile Barry Cornwall chanted the death song of that protective system, but not till gaunt famine, like a ghastly specter, had stalked through the highways and byways of England and Ireland.

In the South cotton was never before or since lower than during part of this period. In New Orleans, the great cotton market of the world, there were, in two days, business failures amounting to nearly thirty millions of dollars. This beats, by heavy odds, the Ryan failure, which has been the talk of Atlanta for a solid month.

Banks suspended or exploded from the lakes to the gulf with a crash as startling as the "crack of doom."

Values of all kinds were greatly depreciated. I saw stalwart negro bucks sold on the block for three and four hundred dollars that in better times brought eight and nine hundred.

The currency away from the money centers consisted of wildcat bank issues, or of shin-plasters, as they were queerly denominated, that in reality were mere promissory notes of private grocers or dry goods merchants. I know a very rich gentleman in this city whose father floated a large amount of these shin-plasters and sustained his commercial credit. This was the exception, most of these issues breaking down in a single season.

But after all, the worst feature of these times was general demoralization in the matter of debt paying.

Stay laws, after the pattern of the thirding laws of a much earlier date, were enacted by State Legislatures. The constitutional provision forbidding a State to pass a law "impairing the obligation of a contract," was either evaded or trampled under foot. On one occasion, the precise date not remembered, I saw a man, afterwards prominent in politics, cudgel another man for bidding at a sheriff's sale—the sheriff for prudential reasons holding his peace. In some communities these judicial sales were either arrested or delayed—the officers of the law being terrorized by the mob.

This state of things obtained with slight improvement until the Harrisburg convention named its candidates— William Henry Harrison, of Ohio, the reputed slayer of Tecumseh, and John Tyler, of Virginia, a State rights Whig. The platform adopted by the Whigs was skillfully adjusted to the financial condition of the country. There was to be a general bankrupt law, embodying both the voluntary and involuntary features. This appeal to the debtor class, who were largely in the ascendancy throughout the nation, caused a widespread enthusiasm.

There was then no demand for the "free coinage of silver," for that metal had not yet been demonetized at the behest of the Wall street plutocrats.

But the Whigs, who were always wise in their generation, had "something better" still to offer in the shape of a national bank, backed by the credit of the General Government. By this measure the people were to realize a happy riddance of the fluctuating currency furnished by the State banks. These two measures were the winning cards in the pending presidential campaign.

The Democratic party of that era seemed smitten with judicial blindness, and their candidate, Mr. Van Buren, was overwhelmingly defeated. Harrison received 234 electoral votes and Van Buren barely sixty.

Thus the national party, which from the days of Jefferson had exercised undisputed sway, met its Waterloo in the campaign of 1840.

Of which dramatic event we shall have something to say at another time.

The Harrison Campaign of 1840.

The popular uprising in the presidential campaign of 1840 was not unlike the present Farmers' Alliance movement, without, however, its grips and passwords. In all the agricultural districts of the country there was then much real or apprehended suffering. The leading products of the farm, as we have previously stated, hardly had any quotable market value. To this must be added the stringency of the money market, and we have not a few of the conditions which have precipitated on the country at this time the Alliance movement and the Ocala platform.

Harrison, the Whig candidate, was trumpeted as the hero of Tippecanoe, but better known to the masses as the "Old Farmer of North Bend."

A *fac simile* of the log cabin in which he lived when Lieutenant Governor of the Northwestern territory was mounted on wheels, gayly decorated with miniature national flags, the clapboard roof ornamented with coonskins, whilst strings of red pepper and a long-handled gourd dangled from the doorposts. The string of the doorlatch was conspicuously on the outside, as an emblem of the proverbial hospitality of the farmer.

On all big occasions, such as barbecues, the log cabin with its trimmings, drawn by Kentucky-raised mules, and driven by a happy-looking plantation darkey, was in place. It was an interesting picturesque scene, not in the shape of high art, but in such shape as best caught the eye and best tickled the fancy of the multitude. Campaign songs, perhaps the model of later negro minstrels, enlivened the occasion and roused the utmost enthusiasm. It may be soberly said that from the banks of the Aristook to the borders of the new-born republic of Texas, the country had gone wild, if not crazy, with political excitement.

We doubt if any single publication of the campaign contributed more to the success of the Whigs than a statistical speech of Congressman Old, of Pennsylvania. The speech was devoted chiefly to an elaborate inventory of the furnishings of the White House. The gold spoons and silver knives and forks—the expensive carpeting—the costly dinner and tea sets—the wine cellars filled with high-priced wine—the extravagance of every kind—was noted and numbered. All this vast outlay for the comfort of Van Buren, the occupant of the White House, whilst the "Old Farmer of North Bend" ate corn dodgers and drank hard cider, and the nation itself trembled on the verge of bankruptcy.

Pamphlet copies of the speech were sown broadcast and knee-deep through the states and territories.

The effect was tremendous, and the movement, which savored strongly of demagogism, developed into a political landslide.

In Georgia, which refused to vote for Van Buren in 1836, it was a one-sided affair. Three of the ablest leaders of the old State-rights' party—Colquitt, Cooper and Black—abandoned their party allegiance and went over to the Van Buren administration. But this was but a ripple on the surface. The bulk of the Whigs, who from the times of Troup and the treaty, had been against what was known as the Union party, stood by their colors and were heavily reinforced from the ranks of the former opposition.

One of the greatest Whig rallies of the campaign in Western Georgia was at Hamilton, Harris county. Not only the people of that county, but hundreds from Troup, Meriwether, Muscogee and Talbot counties, and a large mounted delegation from Chambers county, Alabama, were in attendance. The speakers were Hutchinson and Hilliard, from Montgomery, Ala., Sam Flournoy, from Columbus, and Julius Q. C. Alford, from LaGrange To give greater eclat to the occasion, a military band was brought from Columbus.

The speaking at the grandstand was of the best, and the enthusiasm was immense. Dr. David Cooper, the father of Mrs. Col. N. C. Barnett, was a Whig, warp and filling, and was conspicuous in that vast audience by his stately figure and his hearty applause of the good points scored by the several orators. Col. Wililam C. Osborn, of Hamilton, and his brother, Geo. Osborn, of Waverly Hall, the Farleys, the Walkers, the Mobleys, the Crawfords, the Pitts, and a host of other old Whigs were jubilant.

My first newspaper correspondence was a report of

that meeting to John Forsyth's paper, *The Columbus Times*.

This Whig barbecue was but a specimen brick. All through the State and throughout the country similar scenes were enacted

It is not singular that when, on the kalends of November, the ballots were counted, "Tip and Ty" were found to have won the heat by several lengths, Van Buren barely reaching the distance post.

On the 4th of March, 1841, General Harrison was inaugurated President, and John Tyler, of Virginia, vice-President.

The administration started under bright auspices, but in one month, 4th of April, the President died, the old hero expiring before the acclamations which hailed his inauguration had passed away. His death, however, did not occur until after he had issued an executive proclamation convening Congress in extra session, on the 1st of May. The principal reason assigned in the proclamation for this unusual procedure was the disordered condition of the finances of the country.

President Tyler took the oath of office on the 6th of April, two days after General Harrison's death, and, for the time being everything went smoothly and prosperously with the new regime.

With the assembling of the extra session it was evident that there was discordant elements in the triumphant party.

There was no hitch in the proposed bankrupt law, which gave great relief to the large debtor class of the country. But the project for re-chartering the National Bank met with considerable disfavor, even amongst the friends of the administration.

President Tyler, who was a Virginia statesman of the old school, was not prepared to accept the doubtful policy of re-establishing an institution that originated with Alexander Hamilton, and which, during the forty years of its existence, had produced grave political complications.

His personal opposition to a national bank was an open secret during the late presidential campaign. But his party friends cherished the hope that he would acquiesce to the expressed will of a congressional majority. This he refused to do on two several occasions, and as the majority could not command a two-thirds vote the bank charter failed.

Then followed, as might be supposed, a disruption of the Whig organization. The Harrison cabinet resigned in a body, with the single exception of Mr. Webster, who retained his position with a view to the settlement of the northeastern boundary question with England. It is a singular fact that neither the treaty of Versailles nor the treaty of Ghent adjusted this boundary question. For sixty years its indeterminateness was a perpetual menace to the international relations of both countries. Lord Ashburton and Mr. Webster fixed the boundary to the satisfaction of all concerned.

During the second year of the Tyler administration, 1848, the Dorr insurrection came to a head in the little State of Rhode Island. For nearly two hundred years the charter granted by Charles II. to the trustees of Rhode Island and Providence plantations was the organic law of that commonwealth.

The property qualification demanded of voters had been obnoxious to the poorer classes for many years, and it was the repeal of this feature that Thomas W. Dorr made the basis of his revolutionary procedure. The strife between the "suffrage" and the "law and order" party culminated in riot and bloodshed. Nor was the disturbance quieted until Federal troops were placed at the disposal of Governor King.

Dorr left the State, but was afterwards tried and convicted of treason. He remained in prison for two or more years, and then was unconditionally released.

Another intestine trouble that threatened the peace of the country was anti-rent disturbances in several counties of New York. In Delaware, Renssalaer and Columbia counties the great body of the farmers held only household estates, for the occupancy of which they paid such pepper-corn rents as a day's work or a bushel of oats. But some of them had become weary of this relic of the old Dutch patroonship, and hundreds of them refused to pay the custom any rental. Not satisfied with this, they prohibited other tenants, who were differently disposed, from paying their rents under penalty of being tarred and feathered. In Delaware county these riotous proceedings became frequent and flagrant; so much so, indeed, that Governor Silas Wright declared the county in a state of insurrection, and ordered out the militia to suppress it. This display of the mailed hand soon brought order out of confusion.

The Mormon troubles in Illinois were another feature of Tyler's administration. They were provoked by popular alarm at the rapid spread of this nineteenth century delusion. After milder methods had failed to arrest its progress, a mob broke the jail at Carthage, where Joseph Smith, the Mormon prophet, and his brother Hiram were imprisoned, and assassinated them in cold blood.

Shortly thereafter they fired the Mormon temple at Nauvoo, an act of incendiarism as unwarrantable as the burning of a Catholic convent during the no-popery riots in Boston, and the later destruction of three Catholic churches during the Know-nothing riots in Philadelphia.

The Mormons set forth in a few months for their present home in Utah, where they now number nearly two hundred thousand.

One event, far less dramatic than those we have just glanced at, was pre eminently the crowning glory of this presidential term. We refer to the first notable success of the magnetic telegraph In May, 1844, the National Democratic Convention met in Baltimore, and, after several ballotings, nominated James K. Polk for President and George M. Dallas for Vice-President. The news of this nomination was instantly transmitted to Washington by the Morse telegraph. This was the first message that went over the wires to any considerable distance, and its safe transmission lifted a mountain load from the heart of Prof. Morse, who had been for years the football of fickle fortune and the sport of vulgar wittings.

This message was the signal given for the opening of the most remarkable political campaign during the first century of our national existence. It was the Derby contest of the presidential Newmarket. Clay, the Whig candidate, was, in some respects, the noblest Roman of them all. Theodore Frelinghuysen, the vice-presidential candidate, was the President of the American Bible Society, and, aside from that, was a purely negative quantity.

Polk, the Democratic candidate, was an ex-Speaker of the House, a protege of Jackson, and a thoroughly practical statesman. George M. Dallas was a good second, which led some wag to say that it was a kangaroo ticket, with its main strength in its hind legs.

The next few months were resonant with the booming of the big guns of the platform and the war cries of the rank and file of the two great parties.

The annexation of Texas overshadowed the subordinate issues of bank, tariff and internal improvements.

It was in this connection that Judge Colquitt used to tell his famous story of the "Texas filly," which he claimed had more bottom than "Eclipse," and better speed than "Flying Childers."

When Colquitt brought in this illustration of the immense popularity of the annexation plank of the Democratic platform, the Whigs squirmed and the Democrats yelled.

The result of this contest was that Mr. Clay was shelved, and ceased to be a presidential possibility.

Not only so, but a bill for the annexation of Texas, out of deference to the popular will as expressed at the ballot box, was passed in the closing week of the Tyler administration. We shall have more to say of the lessons of this grand campaign when we come to speak of the Polk and Dallas administration.

THE MEXICAN WAR PERIOD.

We have elsewhere said that the presidential campaign of Clay and Polk, in 1844, was the Derby contest of our national Newmarket. While it was neither so picturesque nor so boisterous as the "Tip and Ty" struggle of 1840, it was by no means wanting in political enthusiasm. It was, in a measure, inaugurated by Mr. Clay's Southern tour in the early spring of that most memorable year. That was the first, and, indeed, last occasion on which I saw the gallant "Harry of the West," and from the platform heard him address an audience of 20,000 people with characteristic force and eloquence. So thrilling were some passages of his speech that they elicited outbursts of applause that almost threatened to rend the welkin.

If personal magnetism had been the dominant issue, the illustrious Kentuckian would have had a walk over. But there were economic questions, such as tariff revision and reduction, which challenged public attention and largely influenced the popular verdict. Beyond all else, however, the annexation question was one that not only appealed to the Southern heart, but likewise to an American sentiment wherever the stars and stripes wantoned with the breeze or shimmered in the mellow sunlight. So strong was this sentiment that weeks and months before the ballots were cast the election of Polk and Dallas was assured.

At this point a brief allusion to the Texan revolution will help us to appreciate the vast popularity of this annexation plank of the Democratic platform. The struggle for Texan independence began in good earnest with the battle of Gonzales in 1835, and, after alarming fluctuations, closed with the decisive battle of San Jacinto in April, 1836. On this historic field independence was achieved and the butchery of the Alamo was signally avenged by the route of the Mexican army and the subsequent capture of its leader, Santa Anna, who lost a leg and a sword in the conflict. The leg, we believe, was buried with the honors of war. The sword was, some years ago, in possession of our old friend, Dr. Borders, of Polk county, the father-in-law of Congressman Everett. Dr. Richardson, of this city, informs me that Dr. Borders has been offered by Texas a large tract of land for the sword, but refuses to part with the relic.

This brilliant victory at San Jacinto was shortly afterwards followed by the recognition of Texan independence by the United States, Great Britain and France, and the "Lone Star Republic" was admitted to the fellowship of the older nations. During the Van Buren administration the Texan government, through its minister at Washington, asked to be incorporated into the Federal Union. This quite natural desire was not then granted, because Mr. Van Buren feared that it might lead to graver political complications with Mexico.

Events were not yet ripe for this "devoutly wished-for consummation." All through the Harrison and Tyler regime the issue was kept in abeyance until the campaign of 1844, when it became an American question of supreme urgency.

When Mr. Polk was inaugurated the marriage union between the sister republics had already been solemnized, not by a treaty, the usual stipulations, but by a joint resolution of the Senate and House of Representatives, approved by the President. One of the first duties of the new administration was to execute the law, and yet it was confronted at the very threshold by a boundary dispute with Mexico. Texas rightfully claimed that her western boundary extended to the Rio Grande. On the other hand, the Mexican government, with Parades at its head, disputed the claim, contending that the Neuces River was the proper western limit of Texas, for the reason that the territory lying between the two rivers appertained to the State of Coahua, which had never shaken off its allegiance to the mother country.

There was a semblance of right in this claim, and the American Government suggested that it be made the subject of negotiation looking to a fair adjustment on some money basis.

Parades, the Mexican President, spurned the proposal, and began massing a large body of troops on the Rio Grande. Thereupon, at the request of the Texas authorities, our Government ordered Colonel Zachary Taylor, a celebrity of the Seminole war, to proceed with

2,000 men to Corpus Christi, at the mouth of the Neuces, and establish at that or some other suitable point a depot of supplies.

This brings us to the first act of the Mexican war drama, the events of which constitute one of the brightest chapters in our national annals.

From the first battle at Palo Alto, May, 1846, where Major Ringgold, a gallant Marylander, poured out his heart's bood as a libation to the goddess of American liberty, to the day General Scott made his triumphal entry into the city of the Montezumas, it was one unbroken series of victories. While it would be wearisome to speak of the minor details of this more than two years of invasion, it is eminently proper to notice the grander movements conducted by Taylor and Scott, who had an equal share in the honors of the struggle.

The first stage of the conflict culminated in the seizure of Monterey in September, 1846, and in the crushing defeat of Santa Anna and his forces at Buena Vista in February of the ensuing year.

It was in this contest, against heavy odds, that our volunteer soldiery demonstrated their admirable fighting qualities and forever silenced the slander that they were mere carpet knights unfitted for the tug of war. It was on this field that our own immortal Davis, who had won his earliest laurels when a junior lieutenant in the Black Hawk war, received imperishable renown by his skillful maneuvering and the stubborn valor of his Mississippi Riflemen in the crisis of the conflict.

As to his peculiar regimental formation it was not a

novelty invented for the occasion, but well known and often practiced amongst the ancient Greeks.

By an order from headquarters the Taylor movement was arrested at Saltillo, a small town beyond Buena Vista.

Santa Anna was in full retreat to the City of Mexico, and a considerable number of Taylor's troops were ordered to reinforce Scott's command, which, having forced the capitulation of that most formidable fortress San Juan D'Ulloa, was marching at no leisurely pace from Vera Cruz upon the enemy's capital. We have always been somewhat incredulous of Prescott's story of the conquest of Mexico by Hernando Cortez. But that wonderful feat, performed by a handful of Spanish cavaliers, with the help of the native Tlascalans, who had revolted against Montezuma, was more than equaled by Scott and his gallant army. From Cerro Gordo, Marion, rocky mountain pass, where the Mexicans made their first bold stand; to Puebla, to Contreras, where Butler and his Palmetto regiment showed themselves worthy descendents of Mexico and Sumter; through Churubusco to the Castle of Chapultepec, from whose flagstaff our own William S. Walker, then a Colonel of Volunteers, unfurled the American flag, thence on to the gates of the city, which they stormed by a bayonet charge, and then to the halls of the Montezumas. Scott's army of the center made no halt, but literally went from "conquering to conquer." We venture to say that neither in Cæsar's "Commentaries," nor in Xenophon's "Anabasis," nor yet in

Napoleon's Italian campaign is there a military record more brilliant than this of our American army. It was in this school that Lee and Jackson and Grant and Sherman and Joe Johnston were trained for their grander achievements in the late civil war.

While Scott was fighting his way to the City of Mexico, smaller detachments of the army and navy, led by Commodore Stockton, Doniphan, Price and Fremont were seizing and occupying the strategic points of New Mexico and California. The Mexicans, beaten from every position, were ready to accept the best terms the conqueror might be willing to grant.

These terms, as embodied in the treaty of Guadaloupe Hidalgo, were generous, even magnanimous, as was befitting the American Government. And yet, as the fruits of the conquest, she acquired an empire in riches and extent, but at the cost of much blood and no inconsiderable treasure.

And yet sectional issues, growing out of these acquisitions, very soon began to embroil the whole country. Scarcely had the treaty been signed until the ghostly specter of discord, threatening the disruption of the Union, appeared in the Wilmot proviso. Freesoilism, as the latest phrase of abolitionism, became a prominent factor in national politics

In the presidential election of 1848, Martin Van Buren was brought forward as the leader of this faction, but the popularity of Taylor and Cass, the Whig and Democratic candidates, held together the old parties, and Mr. Van Buren was a second time distanced on the political race course.

Two measures of vast importance were consummated in the midst of these war disturbances. In its remoter bearings, the principal of these was the settlement of the northwestern boundary between British America and the United States.

For a time the masses of the people of both parties clamored for the parallel of 54.40. But the English government planted itself squarely and in a belligerent attitude on the 49th parallel. Our Mexican embroglio in a degree handicapped the administration. But what finally induced the concession to the English was a conviction on the part of Mr. Calhoun and a large conservative following that an increase of territory in that direction would effectually destroy the equilibrium of the two sections between whom there really then existed but an armed truce. It was in this congressional fight that Henry W. Hilliard, another honored Atlantian, fleshed his maiden sword. This settlement produced a vast outcry in the anti-slavery ranks, some of their leaders denouncing it as an infamous betrayal of our just claim in the interest of the Southern slave-holding barons.

This, however, was the merest partisanship, as England had never claimed less than was finally yielded to her. Hardly secondary to this boundary question was the revision and readjustment of the tariff in conformity to the compromise of 1833.

The whole protection theory was at war with the

THE MEXICAN WAR PERIOD. 111

letter and spirit of the Constitution, and yet, notwithstanding the backset which it received in 1846, the taxpayers of the country are still in the clutches of this terrible octopus.

While we are writing McKinley is making his canvass on the basis of the proposition, either express or implied, that a duty collected at the custom house is not ultimately paid by the American consumer, but by the foreign producers. · To this Mr. Blaine, the great champion of reciprocity, by his indorsement of McKinley, virtually assents. How are the mighty fallen, when Blaine can stultify himself after this fashion! Better creep into his grave or become a tidewaiter, than, for the sake of a cabinet place, to be a party to such a palpable travesty on statesmanship!

It was during the Polk administration that the princely gift of Mr. Smithson, an Englishman, to the United States Government of more than a half million dollars began to be utilized in the interest of science. Under the rectorship of Professor Joseph Henry, formerly of Princeton College, the work has gone forward, resulting in the accumulation of a splendid cabinet of minerals, a large collection of curios and relics, and a laboratory with a splendid chemical equipment. We have seen it stated that there has recently been published "Smithsonian Contributions to Science," in thirty octavo volumes.

On another line, the administration of Polk was made memorable by the gold discoveries of California. Thousands of men, chiefly American citizens, flocked to the Pacific coast in quest of the precious metal. For a season it amounted almost to the *sacra fames auri* of the Latin poet, or in the more expressive language of the time, it reached the proportions of a craze.

It was once feared that the market value of gold would be seriously affected by these mining operations, but the supply has long since diminished and these apprehensions have died out.

In 1848 the Whigs took time by the forelock and nominated General Zachary Taylor, of Louisiana, for the Presidency, and Millard Fillmore, of New York, for the Vice-Presidency.

General Taylor had but little knowledge of statesmanship, but he was an incorruptible patriot, who was widely known and greatly honored as the hero of Okeechobee in the Seminole war and the illustrious victor at Buena Vista. The nomination was hailed everywhere with an enthusiasm that foreshadowed a Whig victory.

Mr. Polk failed to receive a renomination from his party, it being thought advisable to select a Northern man for the Presidency. The choice of the convention fell on General Lewis Cass, a man of great probity of character, with a fair record, both as a warrior and statesman.

The nomination of General Butler, of Kentucky, for the Vice-Presidency, added something to the strength of the Democratic ticket, especially in the West.

Mr. Van Buren's candidacy on the Free-soil ticket drew from the two national parties in about an equal ratio, so that the general result was but slightly affected by this third party movement.

Taylor and Fillmore were chosen by a considerable majority of the electoral votes, and on the 4th of March, 1849, they were both inaugurated without any noteworthy incident.

President Polk retired from his high office with an unblemished reputation, and much honored and beloved by the great body of his fellow countrymen. In like manner Vice-President Dallas had won the respect and confidence of the country, but neither of these excellent officials had those characteristics which rouse popular enthusiasm.

The Compromise Of 1850.

The story of Erostratus, who "fired the Ephesian fane," is one of the most thrilling episodes of ancient history.

So, likewise, during the pendency of the Mexican war period, one David Wilmot, a most incapable Pennsylvania Congressman, hurled a flaming firebrand into our national politics, which ultimately consumed the grander temple of American constitutional liberty.

This incendiary act preceded by more than two years the ratification of the treaty of Guadaloupe Hidalgo. By that treaty our Government acquired an immense territory, stretching across the Rockies to the shores of the Pacific. In the light of subsequent events it was dearly purchased, at the expense of a political conflagration that swept the country, the ashes of which are still warm beneath our tread.

This "Wilmot proviso," which was defeated upon its first presentation in the House of Representatives, was the signal gun of the great civil war. Twenty five years before, the slavery agitation, as respected the national territory, had been laid to rest by the Missouri Compromise. According to the spirit, if not the very letter of that adjustment, the parallel of 36.30 should have been extended through these later territorial acquisitions.

But Mr. Wilmot, with that punic faith which has always characterized his tribe, proposed by a congressional enactment to exclude the Southern people, with their slave property, from this whole territory. This, too, notwithstanding the fact that it had been chiefly acquired by Southern troops under the leadership of Southern commanders.

But beyond this we do not care to speak of that proviso. We are more concerned at present to speak of the great compromise of 1850, which was the supreme effort of conservative statesmanship to eliminate sectional issues from American politics.

This was in no dubious sense the specific work of the Tyler and Fillmore administrations.

In December, 1849, at San Jose, the people of California organized a State Government, under a Constitution prohibitory of slavery. At the same time they forwarded a petition to Congress for their admission to the dignity of statehood. This petition elicited a memorable debate, in which the great lights of the American Senate—Clay, Calhoun and Webster—were quite naturally most conspicuous.

Mr. Calhoun, we believe, in February, 1850, caused to be read by his Senatorial colleague a masterly speech in defense of Southern rights. It was in the best spirit, as was befitting the dignity of the forum and his own eminent statesmanship. And now his political career was ended, and he retired gracefully from the arena of his former triumphs.

In March following, Mr. Webster delivered the grandest oration of his life. He rose far above the level of a vulgar partisanship, and not a few of his utterances were like the echoes of Sinaitic thunder, when even Moses quaked and feared exceedingly.

He appealed to his own native New England for the exercise of a broader patriotism, with a glow of fancy and a sweep of thought that challenged the admiration of the civilized world. He, too, like Calhoun and Clay, was nearing immortality, and yet for these words, that were inspirational in their loftiness of conception and sublimity of patriotic purpose, he was shut out from Faneual hall, the boasted cradle of American liberty.

Matters had reached a crisis when, on May 6th, Mr. Clay himself appeared for the last time in his favorite role of the "great pacificator," as chairman of a committee of thirteen, selected to prepare a basis of settlement for all the sectional issues growing out of our recent acquisitions of territory.

The first section of the bill, better known as the Omnibus Bill, assured to Texas the right to organize four States out of her territory, with or without slavery, as the inhabitants thereof might elect; the next section authorized the admission of California, with her recently adopted Constitution prohibiting slavery or involuntary servitude; the third section provided for the organization of New Mexico and Utah as Territories, without slavery restriction; the fourth provided for a more rigid enforcement of the constitutional provision for the rendition of fugitive slaves. The last section abolished the slave trade in the District of Columbia, under heavy penalties. These provisions seemed to cover all the points in controversy. During the next few months this compromise was debated with great ability in both houses of Congress, as well as in all parts of the Union.

In Georgia it was injected into local politics, and the matter thoroughly canvassed in county and district meetings. It led, moreover, to a partial disruption of the old Democratic party. In Georgia, Howell Cobb and John H. Lumpkin, representing the Rome and Athens districts in Congress, headed the Union Democrats, and by a coalition with the Whigs carried the gubernatorial election of 1851, defeating Charles J. McDonald and electing Howell Cobb. This estrangement, however, between the Union and State Rights Democrats was of short duration. A large majority of the former returned to the Democratic fold, and in 1853, Herschel V. Johnson was chosen over Charles J. Jenkins by a meager majority.

That small majority had, however, more than a temporary significance. It showed the increasing strength of the secession sentiment in the old commonwealth. Nor is it improbable that if the Constitutional Unionists had succeeded in 1853, that Georgia would not have passed an ordinance of secession, and that means we would have had no war between the States.

But we have no space for these dubious speculations.

Pending the great debate in Congress, President Taylor succumbed to a sudden but mortal illness, and Mr. Fillmore, taking the oath of office, placed his hand upon the helm of government.

The compromise measures, without material amendment, were adopted in September by both houses of Congress and approved by the President. A temporary lull followed this pacific adjustment, but the agitation was renewed after a short breathing spell in a fiercer form than had been previously witnessed.

Several of the Northern States enacted personal liberty bills, under the auspices of what they were pleased to term the "higher law." Thus seeking under color of a moral sanction to frustrate the constitutional provision for the rendition of fugitive slaves, and in like manner to invalidate the recent compromise. As might be supposed, this striking exhibition of bad faith fanned the flames of discord in the South, and for the first time not a few of the more conservative statesmen of that section began to calculate seriously the value of a union with states that neither respected the fundamental law nor the acts of Congress framed for its enforcement.

During the remainder of Fillmore's official term there were minor incidents, such as the ill-starred Lopez expedition for the conquest of Cuba. With a handful of reckless adventurers like himself, he sailed from New Orleans without adequate equipment, and effected a landing on the island to find himself received with scant courtesy by the Cubans, whose liberation was the avowed object of the invasion. He likewise found himself confronted with a large body of Spanish troops, who speedily captured the leader of the expedition and his principal followers and brought them to Havana, where they were summarily executed.

This affair induced a proposal from the English and French Governments for a tripartite treaty that would have forever barred the American Government from the acquisition of Cuba. Mr. Everett, the Secretary of State, refused outright to accept the proposal, and took occasion in his diplomatic correspondence to reaffirm the Monroe doctrine.

Another event of widespread interest was the visit of Louis Kossuth, the Hungarian leader in the revolution of 1852. This revolutionist was welcomed by large audiences in the principal American cities, and considerable sums were contributed to the exhausted exchequer of the countrymen of Maria Theresa. The immediate results were small, but there can be no doubt that the original movement, headed by Kossuth and shamefully betrayed to its undoing by the infamous Georgey, led at a later period to the formation of the existing Austro-Hungarian empire.

The time had now arrived when the two great American parties were again to measure their strength in a presidential struggle. The main fight was to be conducted on the compromise of 1850, from which patriotic settlement the Northern Whigs had already receded. This was shown in the National Whig Convention of 1852, in which Fillmore was incontinently shelved. While it is true that the convention indorsed those measures in their platform by a heavy majority, yet their repudiation of Mr. Fillmore clearly indicated their hostility to that principal measure of his administration. Gen. Scott, whose military reputation was unsurpassed, was chosen for the first place on their ticket. The Democrats likewise indorsed the compromise of 1850, and presented as their representative Franklin Pierce, of New Hampshire, and W. R. King, of South Carolina. Neither of these were conspicuous, either for military or civil renown, but the dissensions in the Whig party, growing out of anti-slavery sentiment, gave them the vantage ground in the contest. That sentiment had waxed stronger, especially in the rural districts of the North and West, until the party of Clay and Webster had been sorely disintegrated, and was already verging on dissolution.

And this very naturally suggests the fact that Henry Clay and Daniel Webster both died in 1852, only two or three months intervening between the departures of these illustrious statesmen. These, with John C. Calhoun, formed the brightest political constellation in the political firmament, and might be well likened to the three Empyreal suns that blazed in the "belt of Orion." All of these died during Fillmore's administration, a coincidence that will render it famous through all generations. Other great men will arise from time to time, for as yet our country has not " lost the breed of noble bloods."

But we do not exaggerate when we say that not for a thousand years will another such triumvirate arise to adorn the Senate Chamber, where are gathered the representatives of sovereign States.

Greek history records but one age of Pericles; English history but one Elizabethan era; French history but one imperialism like that of Louis Quatorze, and American history may never chronicle another epoch equal to that of Clay, Calhoun and Webster.

Great Pulpit Orators.

John Newland Maffit.

We have lying on our table an old book printed at New London, Conn., in 1821. It is an autobiography written by the distinguished minister whose name stands at the head of this sketch.

Fifty years ago Mr. Maffit was one of the pulpit celebrities of the Methodist church. As an orator he was classed with such men as Durbin, Bascom and George Pierce. He was a native of Ireland, having been born in Dublin in 1794. His parents, he tells us, belonged to the Methodist "society," but were "rigidly attached to the established church." This statement sounds odd enough to the uninitiated who do not know that in its earliest years Methodism was not so much a church as a religious association, within the pale of the English church. For a long time its Sabbath services were not held during canonical hours, and its ministers and members received the sacraments at the hands of the clergy of the establishment.

John Wesley, the immortal founder, had what savored of a superstitious dread of schism. He feared nothing so much unless it was the devil, about whose personality he entertained not even the shred of a doubt. It was the work and weariness of his last years to prevent a separation which he clearly foresaw was inevitable after his death, and which he provided for in that famous legal document, the "Deed of Declaration," which he enrolled in the Court of Chancery in 1784.

In this faith, pure and simple, Mr. Maffit was brought up by his pious parents, and yet he confesses that for a few years he was wayward and reckless in no ordinary degree. His conversion, of which he has furnished full details in this autobiography, bears a close resemblance to that of John Bunyan and the later John Newton. Religion amongst the old Methodists and the older Puritans, was not an evolution but a cataclysm. The line of cleavage between the old and the new was abrupt. Maffit had his share of visions and wrestlings, and hand to hand conflicts with Apollyon in the valley of humiliation. Let not the beardless theologians of the present generation mock these experiences of the fathers.

There may have been a bit of superstition and a greater amount of subjectiveness in all this, but when they were converted it was from head to heel and from center to circumference. It made them the moral heroes who went forth to the spiritual conquest of the American wilderness and the moral uplifting of the Cornish miners and the weavers and spinners of Manchester and the sailors of the London and Liverpool dockyards.

It gave Asbury and McKendree to America, Gideon Ousley to Ireland and John Nelson and a score like him to England. Shortly after his conversion Maffit sailed for America, where he was destined to find a wide field for the exercise of his marvelous gifts as a preacher.

Before leaving his native land, however, he had some novel experiences as a street preacher, being jeered and occasionally rotten-egged, and other such treatment as the Salvation Army of to-day receives from the hoodlums and gutter snipes of our populous centers. On one occasion he attempted to break up a ball by a stirring exhortation, followed by an enthusiastic prayer. For this misplaced and ill-timed zeal he got much ridicule, and narrowly escaped a broken head.

Upon his arrival in America he found that Methodism had better social recognition than in Ireland, and in some of the Middle States had rooted itself in the higher strata of the population.

Adjusting himself to his altered environment, he laid aside his more aggressive methods and cultivated a pulpit style not unlike that of Milburn, the blind Chaplain of the House of Representatives, and only a shade more exuberant in fancy than that of John Summerfield.

Dr. Hoss, of Nashville, in his admirable ecumenical address on the religious press, says of Maffit that "he was an Irishman and an orator, two words that mean the same thing." This is true, but it must not be forgotten that Ireland has distinct schools and grades of oratory. Burke and Curran were both Irish orators, but the former was ponderous—the latter indulged in flights of fancy that suited better the jury room than the House of Commons. Maffit in the pulpit had a striking resemblance to Curran at the bar, by no means so classical and yet the same nimble fancy and a diction equally gorgeous. We never heard Mr. Maffit preach, nor did he leave a volume of sermons, so that we are compelled to rely on traditional accounts, which are vague and unsatisfactory. A very dear friend of ours listened to a series of sermons delivered by Mr. Maffit at Albany, N. Y., far back in the thirties. At that time, this friend, since greatly distinguished on the bench, was a law student in the office of Hon. Ogden Hoffman. He was himself a man of thorough culture and decided gifts as an elocutionist. He spoke of Maffit as a charming preacher, whose delivery was faultless, and whose word painting was unrivalled by any minister to whom he had then listened. He was able to recall some passages that thrilled me in the recital, but which have dropped out of my own memory.

But this matters little, as this friend's testimony was borne by all his contemporaries. Dr. Lovick Pierce also put a high estimate on Mr. Maffit's ability as a preacher. At one period of his life Mr. Maffit was chosen editor of the *Nashville Advocate*, no mean compliment to any writer.

His latter years were saddened and shadowed by bodily affliction. Nor is it amiss to say that he suffered from other causes that we do not care to dwell upon. To his dying day he retained the affection and confidence of thousands who trusted implicitly in his ministerial and personal integrity, believing him to be the victim of persecution. He died, and is buried at Mobile, Alabama, much loved and honored in that center of Alabama Methodism.

Mr. Maffit left several sons, one of whom was a gallant captain of our Confederate navy, and a bosom friend of that old "sea lion," Admiral Semmes, and of his right bower, Captain Kell, the Adjutant General of Georgia. Another of his sons, now dead, was the husband of Mrs. Maffit, of this city. That late noble Christian woman, Mrs. B. B. Crew, was his grand daughter. One of Dr. Maffit's daughters was the wife of Mirabeau B. Lamar, the second President of Texas. Others of Atlanta, and Mobile's worthiest citizens are related to this eminent minister by marriage or consanguinity.

I had hoped to find, in the book to which I alluded in the outset, some specimens of his pulpit productions, but it was written while he was quite young, twenty-five years of age—and still we detect in his pious reflections, scattered throughout the volume, the buddings of that genius which in after years made him a most attractive and able minister of the gospel.

In his youth he seems at intervals to have paid court to the "tuneful nine." Some of the first fruits are found in several short poems which constitute an appendix to his autobiography. They remind us of the earlier poems of Henry Kirke White, having about them the same religious fervor and flavor. As they are the immature products of his younger years, they are not to be tried by the canons of a sterner criticism. They, doubtless, would have a charm for many readers.

Henry Biddleman Bascom.

Dr. Bascom was a sharp contrast to the eminent minister just sketched. He was a native of New York, but from an early age was identified with Southern Methodism.

When a mere strippling he entered the ministry, first in Ohio, afterwards in Kentucky, where his ministerial fortunes were strangely checkered. He was, when still young, a man of majestic features and figure, with a Jovian brow and an eye to "threaten and command." He affected fine clothes, which, amongst not a few of his clerical contemporaries, was esteemed a grievous fault. His style of speech in the pulpit subjected him to censure, and not a few "plain, packstaff Methodists" amongst the laity and a goodly number of the old-fashioned elders in the ministry, greatly feared that the youthful orator was a bit too self-conceited.

It was, therefore, considered a wise policy to send the young preacher to mountain circuits, where the rough and tumble experiences of itinerant life would take the starch out of his clerical vestments. But young Bascom had "the root of the matter" in him, and came forth from the ordeal strengthened in purpose and in far better repute with preachers and people.

It was a lucky chance for Bascom that brought him to the knowledge of Henry Clay. Mr. Clay was charmed with his conversation and preaching, and is credited with saying that he had no equal in the American pulpit. This indorsement of the Kentucky giant gave

Bascom the *entree* to the best circles and the foremost positions in the Methodist church.

In a few years he was chosen as a delegate to the General Conference, where he was destined to win greater distinction.

In the memorable conference of 1844, he was in some respects the most conspicuous of the Southern delegates in that body of representative men. As a debater he made no considerable figure, being overshadowed by such trained disputants as Winans, of Mississippi; Capers, of South Carolina; Smith and Early, of Virginia, and Paine, of Tennessee. But when it came to the appointment of some one to prepare the protest of the Southern minority, Bascom was selected for that purpose, and discharged that duty with marked ability.

In the Louisville Convention of the next year (1845), which organized the M. E. Church South, on the basis of the plan of separation adopted the previous year by the General Conference, his valuable services were again in requisition. He it was that prepared a paper setting forth the reasons for separation—a document which in clearness of statement and vigor of argument compares favorably with Webster's letter to Baron Hulseman.

Dr. Bascom, because of his scholarly attainments, was at different times made president of two or more colleges and universities.

At the second General Conference held at St. Louis in 1850, Dr. Bascom was elected to the Episcopacy. Contrary to immemorial custom he was designated to preach his own ordination sermon. That grandest effort of his ministry gave assurance that in his new and responsible position he would be a blessing to the church which had so highly honored him. But his Episcopal career was cut short by an untimely death, having, we believe, presided at but a single session of an annual conference.

Leaving these brief biographical details, we proceed to speak of his characteristics as a pulpit orator.

We have already remarked that Maffit and Bascom were sharply contrasted in their pulpit styles. The former had a larger share of the *"suaviter in modo,"* and with more fancy had less of the Miltonic imagination. Bascom, in consequence of his better educational advantages, was more classical and more logical. But we question if he was the equal of Maffit in the ability to melt and move a vast assembly. In Bascom there was more of that majestic bearing and intellectual sweep which was seen in Thomas Chalmers when he thundered from the pulpit of the Ton church, and in some wise shook Scotland from Maiden Kirk to John O'Groats.

Bascom loved the great themes of Revelations. He liked to toy with thunderings and lightnings of Sinai and to portray in vivid colors the scenes of the general judgment. When standing on these loftier altitudes of Christian thought he was as much at home as the eagle when he spurns some Alpine summit and soars right onward and upward to the sun.

Bishop Bascom published several volumes of college lectures, and we believe but a single volume of sermons.

These latter have been widely read and much admired by the younger Methodist clergy, and some of them have been so inconsiderate as to attempt to imitate Bascom's pulpit methods. It is the old story of the stripling David in Saul's armor, but some of them were not as wise as the son of Jesse, who put aside the battle harness of the stalwart Benjaminite and went forth to the combat with his shepherd's sling and a few stones gathered out of the wayside brook.

But we recur to his ordination sermon at St. Louis in 1850 as his masterpiece. Demosthenes made many wonderful orations, but none of them was equal to the "Oration on the Crown." Bascom likewise preached a number of great sermons, but in none of them did he reach the high water mark of his genius, except in that notable discourse. The text was: "God forbid that I should glory, save in the cross of our Lord Jesus Christ." Of course the burden of the sermon was the atonement. It happily blended argument and appeal. It was logic at a white heat. It was eloquence such as might become the tongue of an angel who, returning from an errand to some far-off planet, hovered for a brief while on poised wing above reprobate Jerusalem, and was an eye-witness of the crucifixion. So thrilling was the sermon that gray-haired veterans wept like children, and some shouted "Hosannah to the Son of David!"

The peroration was a climax of beauty and power. We can only recall it in part. Said the newly elected bishop: "When we speak of the cross we do not refer to that symbol of redemption as it blazed on the imperial labarum of Constantine, nor yet as it appeared in the mystic monogram of the Rosicrucian, but that divine cross of Calvary, all stained with hallowed blood, which is the sign and seal of a world's redemption. Let its precious light go forth to the ends of creation, until from every dwelling place of universal being there shall be heard the loud acclaim: "The cross! The cross!! The cross!!!"

Character Sketches.

John the Beloved Disciple.

It requires no inconsiderable stretch of fancy to conceive of the aged presbyter of Ephesus who wrote the charming Epistles to Gaius and to the elect lady as once "a mere boy playing beside his father's boat on that bright strip of sand which still marks the site of Bethsaida." And yet even the average human life from youth to extreme age is full of such varied and rare, we might say such incongruous incidents and experiences.

The especial pre-eminence of St. John in the apostolic college was in a large measure due to the fact that he was "the disciple whom Jesus loved." There is little force in the suggestion that possibly there was a bit of nepotism in the ardent attachment of our Saviour to the younger son of Zebedee and Salome. While the Master and His favorite disciple were kinsmen by birth and blood, yet we feel assured that their close and confidential relationship was not the simple out-growth of an unreasoning human sentiment, but rather the result of a spiritual kinship as indicated by their striking moral affinity.

While Peter and James shared with John the stronger confidence and warmer fellowship of their divine leader, yet even in this inner circle of discipleship there were unmistakable evidences that he stood foremost in rank as he did in gifts and graces.

In the first general council at Jerusalem, St. Paul—whether by a wise intuition or by a direct revelation is of no great consequence—readily perceived that these three were reckoned pillar Apostles. They constituted a sort of *imperium in imperio;* and, strangely enough as we see it, naming them as James, Cephas and Joseph, he inverted the order in which we are inclined to place them. This, if intentional on the part of St. Paul, might be accounted for by the circumstance that on this particular occasion James, the titular and perhaps rightful bishop of the mother Church, presided over the council, and that Peter, as was his habit, was the chief speaker John, as on other occasions, was reticent because, as some have conjectured, of a becoming deference to his older brethren of the apostleship.

But perhaps a better clue to the habitual reserve of this great apostle is furnished by Archdeacon Farrar. He states that St. John was of a contemplative habit, and, therefore, did not affect the more aggressive methods of his fellow-apostles. Not one of them, however, was his equal in culture or social position, nor did any of them contribute as largely to the literature of the New Covenant. That John was justified in referring to himself by the modest circumlocution as "the disciple whom Jesus loved" is evident from two recorded incidents of the Last Supper. The circumstance of his leaning on the breast of Jesus was probably not exceptional; at any rate, it was significant. Nor was it less so when Simon Peter would know who of their number would betray him that the Master made this same disciple the medium of communication to the other brethren. The clearest proof, however, of the Saviour's firm trust in John's personal fidelity was at the crucifixion. Forgetting the agonies he was suffering, losing sight of the mockings and revilings of the Priest-ridden rabble that swayed to and fro at the foot of the cross, he sought the eager eye of the beloved disciple, and said: "Son, behold thy mother." Henceforth the blessed Virgin became the honored and cherished guest of the beloved disciple.

This is but a single instance of the responsiveness of John to the slightest word or wish of the Master. Just as the strings of the harp were responsive to the softest finger touch of the stripling David, so every chord of John's heart was adjusted to the faintest whisper of Christ's love. Psychologists talk long and learnedly of persons that are *en rapport* one with the other. This mysterious relationship does exist, and it was in no dubious sense a bond of endearment between the Saviour and his apostle.

But, if we analyze the character of St. John, we discover that beyond any and all others of that immediate generation, he combined those qualities which shone brightest in the character and life of the world's Redeemer. These qualities were a tenderness more than womanly, and a courage that neither quaked nor quailed in the presence of difficulty or danger.

The familiar couplet,

> The bravest are the tenderest,
> The loving are the daring.

was illustrated in the character of St. John. That he was gentle in a remarkable degree was abundantly shown in many incidents of his life, and yet more strikingly in the Fourth Gospel and in his three Epistles. It must have been a warm and loving heart from which leaped, like an altar-flame, that loftiest generalization of Holy Writ: "God is love." Who, indeed, can compass its manifold and marvelous meanings? How it puts to shame every other theism, oriental or occidental! How it brings

> Joy to the desolate; Light to the straying!

Ay, more, how it opens the door of hope in every "Valley of Achor!" and how it whispers to every chafed spirit and troubled heart the "Peace be still" which caused the waves of Gennesaret to crouch obediently at the feet of the incarnated word and wisdom of God! O, my disquieted soul, hope thou in God, for His nature and His name is love. A love passing the love of woman, whether wife or mother; a love that flares forth at midnight through the deep defiles and up the dizzy steeps of dark mountains, searching diligently for the lost sheep and bringing it back to the shelter of the fold.

John, beyond any of the apostles, has firmly grasped this central idea of the gospel. Hence, in his own gospel, he hurries away from the mystery of the Logos and lingers long and lovingly on the valedictory sayings of his Master, where there is much of the Comforter and the "house of many mansions" and the abiding peace and the perennial joy that remaineth.

There was, however, another side to the character of this great apostle. He was not, as a distinguished writer has said, the dreamful "pietest which appears in the pictures of Titian and Raphael." At times, not a few, he manifested that "Elijah spirit" which made the Saviour characterize him as a "Son of Thunder"—less impulsive, it may be, than Peter, but when fully roused more vehement. It was this "manner of spirit," moreover, which made him, on the night of the betrayal, enter boldly into the palace of the high priest when the other ten, taking no account of Iscariot, faltered and fled or followed afar off like Simon Peter. Nor did Peter's denial, of which he was in some sort an eye and ear witness, in the least shake the constancy of his steadfast mind. All through the hours of that night of tenebrific blackness did he, like Abdiel, the stripling seraph of "Paradise Lost," keep his loyalty untarnished.

On the next day this unswerving loyalty was further shown when he was the sole representative of the apostolate in that group of devoted women who stood in the shadow of the cross. To his presence we owe our knowledge of one striking feature of that tragic scene. We allude to the brutal spear-thrust of the Roman soldier, in response to which blood and water issued forth, testifying to the certainty of his death, and typical of the cleansing and saving power of that death.

But the greater displays of John's sterner nature were

reserved to his riper years, when he endured the utmost stress of Jewish and Roman persecution.

The legend of the caldron of boiling oil from which he escaped unhurt may have no historic basis, but there is no sufficient reason to question the story of his banishment by an edict of Domitian to Patmos, a barren rock in the Ægean Sea. There it was that he "saw the Apocalypse," with its wild and weird imagery. There it was that he witnessed the opening of the seven seals and heard the blast of the seven trumpets as they sounded the march of the Christian centuries toward the final consummation. Away from the habitations of men and shut out from the communion of saints, he was granted a vision of the glorified church—a great multitude redeemed out of every kindred, tongue and people.

In this sea-girt prison he is thought to have written the Revelation and most probably his First Epistle. Some have likewise suggested that during this enforced loneliness he wrote the Fourth Gospel, in which he supplies the notable "lack of service" of the Synoptists. This would leave only his brief Second and Third Epistles for his later residence at Ephesus, the capitol of Proconsular Asia. There is, however, much confusion in the chronology of that period, so that there is no great degree of certitude in these statements. Besides, there are some marks of a controversial aim in both his Gospel and First Epistle, which would place them at a later date.

His Episcopal residence at Ephesus, to which we

have just referred, although well established as a fact, is shrouded in mystery. Many things are related of these closing years of the "beloved disciple" that have been greatly questioned. The story of his reclaiming an apostate youth from a life of brigandage is a romantic feature of these later years, and is so thoroughly characteristic of the great apostle that we are reluctant to discredit it. So we might say of the beautiful incident of his being borne in his Episcopal chair to the assemblies of the Ephesian Church, and with tremulous voice and uplifted hands, exhorting them: "Little children, love one another." But after all, the most curious myth was one which was based on the response of the Saviour to the impertinent questioning of Peter in regard to the destiny of John: "What if I will that he tarry until I come?"

This response raised a general expectation amongst the disciples that John would survive the second advent; and yet it was as the scriptures teach, a palpable misinterpretation. Here it may be, however, we have the germ of the legend of the Wandering Jew, who, under various names, as Ahasuerus, Salathiel, and others, "has passed like night from land to land."

Be this as it may, yet, sooner or later, the hour struck when the last apostle must needs die—not, as in the case of the other eleven, by violence, but, as was befitting the character of John, in quietness and in the midst of gentle ministrants, human and angelic,

> While heaven and earth conspired to say
> How blest the righteous when he dies.

St. James, Bishop of Jerusalem.

CONSERVATISM—a ponderous word, whether in politics or religion—is the term that best expresses the leading characteristics of James, "the Lord's brother," and the first Bishop of Jerusalem.

In a technical sense, James was a non-apostolic man, like Luke, the evangelist, and Barnabas, the "son of consolation." And yet, in a broader acceptation, he was reckoned one of the three "pillar apostles" by the mother Church at Jerusalem.

In what sense he was our "Lord's brother" is involved in some obscurity. If literally true, it overthrows the Catholic dogma of the perpetual virginity of the blessed mother of Christ. With such speculations, which are more curious than edifying, we have no present concern. That James was a Nazarite from his birth, and that he was reared to manhood in the house of Joseph and Mary at Nazareth, are as well ascertained as any other facts in connection with the holy family.

Such an environment was favorable to the development of every human virtue, and James grew to man's estate greatly respected and beloved by all classes of his Jewish countrymen. Although a devoted disciple of Jesus, he was, by reason of his strict observance of the Mosaic laws, in good repute with the hierarchy at Jerusalem, so much so, indeed, that they surnamed him "The Just."

The best analysis of the character of James may be soonest arrived at by a careful study of his General

Epistle, which, according to our conception, is a sort of connecting link between the Old and New Testament Scriptures. It was not formally admitted into the sacred canon until the Council of Carthage, A. D. 394. Previously, however, it had been accepted by the Syrian Church and incorporated into the Peshito, one of the earliest versions of which we have any knowledge. Whilst several of the Fathers rejected it, others of these—including the learned Latin Father Jerome—gave it their indorsement as thoroughly canonical. That the Epistle was known to the Church at a very early period abundantly appears from the fact that St. Peter, as shown in his First Epistle, was familiar with its text. Some of the thoughts, and even verbiage, of St. Peter particularly, as it relates to the disciplinary uses of adversity, are almost identical with those of St. James.

The most striking peculiarity of this Epistle is the emphasis with which the apostle stresses the observance of the moral law in order to personal salvation. It was this salient feature that made it a stone of stumbling to Luther, and induced him to stigmatize it as a "straw Epistle," quite unworthy of a place in the sacred canon. This alleged discrepancy as to the mode of human justification between the teachings of Paul and James was indeed a favorite topic of discussion with the schoolmen of the Middle Ages. For centuries these exegetes were puzzling themselves and mystifying their readers as well, about a matter which, like the question of the harmony of the Gospels, only needed the research and scholarship of a later age to adjust in a manner eminently satisfactory to the great body of Christian believers.

Fortunately for the peace and sound indoctrination of the Church, neither the Pauline nor the Jacobean view has prevailed to the utter exclusion of the opposite view. "Not of works, lest any man should boast," is true; so, likewise, that other saying: "Knowest thou not, O vain man, that faith without works is dead, being alone?" These, as has often been argued, are complementary truths, and in no just sense contradictory doctrinal statements. The rejection of the former entangles us with a legal issue which is of the very essence of Pharisaism, while the rejection of the latter would entail on the Church the curse of Antinomianism. In either event our theology would be warped and of necessity lopsided. But, by a reconcilement of the two Apostles —really a matter of little difficulty—we reach a conclusion in perfect accord with the analogy of the faith.

It would be a grave injustice to lay to the charge of either the palpable perversions and even monstrous errors which have been propounded and practiced under color of authority of one or the other.

Whilst it is well understood that the Epistles to the Romans and Galatians have been distorted by Antinomians, to the serious hurt of Christianity, so likewise the Epistle of St. James has been twisted—or, rather, travestied—by legalists to the great hinderance of Gospel truth. But St. Paul is no whit responsible for the folly of Solfidianism, nor is St. James chargeable with the not less mischievous heresy of Ebionism. The effort of the Council of Trent to straddle the issue is at best a "most lame and impotent conclusion," which needs no refutation at our hands. It occurs to us that St. James himself covers the whole field of this unseemly wrangle when he characterizes the Gospel as "a perfect love of liberty." This by any fair interpretation shuts out error in both directions. The Gospel is not a bare euphemism, but a law as stringent as that which the Divine finger wrote on the two stone tables of Sinai. Both are the work of the same "legislative God." Both have for their sanctions nothing less than eternal life or endless death. And yet that "perfect law" brings deliverance from a bondage more cruel than abolitionism ever feigned or fancied in the rice-fields of the Carolinas or on the sugar estates of Louisiana. It proclaims a moral liberty to the captive of sin untainted by license—a liberty to be won not by the mailed hand of controversy, but received by the broken heart and contrite spirit of penitence.

Some have been inclined to weaken the authority of the Epistle on the ground that the Gospel is not once named in the five chapters that compose it. A like criticism as to shallowness was long ago made on the Book of Esther, because, forsooth, the name of God is not mentioned a single time by its author, whether Ezra or Nehemiah. The oft-quoted reply to this objection that in no book of the Old Testament are the foot-prints and finger-marks of a Divine Providence more clearly visible, at once effectually silences the puerile cavil.

That St. James wrote his Epistle to antagonize the special views of St. Paul, and in the interest of the Judaizing teachers who so stoutly opposed him in his apostolic work, has scarcely the semblance of historic truth.

The probabilities are largely in favor of the theory that the Epistle antedates the period of the "foolish Galatians," as well as the weightier Epistle to the Romans. Moreover, the personal relations between Paul and James, as shown from the former's successive visits to Jerusalem, contraindicate the correctness of this statement. The one as the representative of Judaic Christianity, and the other as the representative of Gentile Christianity, at no time or place had a "sharp contention," as did Paul and Barnabas at Antioch. Whatever their minor differences, they both, in the best of moods, went their several ways, both aiming at the glory of God and the honor of a common Saviour.

From this polemical writing we turn to the simpler and more congenial study of the manner of the life and death of the first Bishop of Jerusalem. The religious life of St. James was somewhat tinged by an asceticism that savored of the sect of the Essenes, whose scheme of philosophy was the stoicism of Hebrew history.

By some writers he has been likened to John the Baptist, whose trumpet-voice first roused a backslidden people to a consciousness of their individual and national transgressions. Beyond any man of the first century, St. James was abundant in fastings and prayers. Of the latter it has been said that such was the frequency of his public and private devotions that his knees were "worn hard like those of a camel."

He had the same love for the sanctuary that distinguished the aged Simeon and Anna the prophetess, who departed not from the temple day or night. While St. Paul owed to him the earliest official recognition of Gentile Christianity, yet it is doubtful if St. James ever was outside of the walls of Jerusalem after the ascension of Christ. Nor did this proceed from any indifference to the evangelistic work of Peter and Paul, but from a thorough conviction that Jerusalem—the Holy City—was the divinely-appointed field of his apostolic labor. There was about him a brotherly appreciation of moral goodness, wherever seen, that endeared him to all classes of his countrymen. Already we have referred to the fact that because of the immaculate purity of his life he was surnamed "The Just," to which popular verdict even the stern ecclesiasticism of the Scribes assented.

But soon the shadows began to thicken about James and the city he so ardently loved. As the day of reckoning drew near, there were portents and prophecies of the impending destruction. During the Feast of Tabernacles, and likewise in the midst of the Paschal solemnities, a wild-eyed fanatic, called Jesus, appeared upon the scene. He was only a less mysterious personage than Melchizedek, who met Abraham after his slaughter of the five kings. Day and night he lifted up his voice in wailing and warning. The little children were nestled closer to their mothers, as the stillness of midnight was broken by his frantic outcry: "Woe to Jerusalem! woe to the Temple!"

By every visible token a mightier and sharper sword than that of Damocles was suspended above the Davidic capital, which, like majestic Babylon, had made itself drunken with the "blood of the saints." Already the tramp of the Roman legions might be heard in the dim distance. The prophetic eagles were gathering to the carcass of a doomed city and a dead dispensation. But despite these evil omens the rush of traffic and the revelry of licentiousness suffered not even a momentary abatement. "As it was in the days of Noah so also shall it be in the days of the Son of man." These words spake Jesus as He departed from the Temple, and now they were to be shortly fulfilled. At this critical juncture the Sanhedrim hierarchy that "sat in Moses' seat" began to plot for the murder of the saintly Christian Bishop of Jerusalem. Under the leadership of Hanan, a descendant of the wicked Caiphas of our Saviour's time, they secured the arrest of James, and, placing him on the pinnacle of the Temple, they mocked and jeered him, and closed the shameful spectacle by hurling him down headlong. Seeing that he was not killed by the fall they began to stone him, as aforetime they had stoned the blessed martyr Stephen. In the midst of the murderous melee St. James scrambled to his knees and prayed, saying: "I entreat thee, O Lord God! O, Father, forgive them, for they know not what they do." Thereupon a Rechabite of priestly rank entreated the rabble to spare the "just one." But, instead, one of their number seized a fuller's club and smote out the brains of the venerable servant of God. They buried him, we are told, beside the sanctuary he had loved long and well.

Josephus was not alone in the belief that this killing of St. James was one of the principal causes of the destruction of Jerusalem. At any rate, it was the beginning of an end that was tragical beyond precedent or parallel.

If the martyrdom of St. James occurred, as is most probable, in the year 63, then short shrift was granted that untoward generation. Seven years thereafter the destruction of the city was completed. Not only was the Temple burned to the ground, but its foundations were upturned by the plowshares, the walls of the city were leveled, and its gates dismantled. Such of its inhabitants as escaped the sword and the pestilences and the famine were "parted and scattered" to the ends of the earth. The nobler captives were reserved to grace the triumph at Rome, but many thousands were sold into abject slavery. By such methods did the Most High avenge the quarrel of His violated covenant.

But after all, this terrible destruction was "the bringing in of a better hope." Christian Judaism, as inculcated by St. James, would have been of necessity provincial. Like Mohammedanism, it would have been no less than Buddhism or Brahmanism, one of the ethnic religions of the world. Christianity must have a wider area and a broader field for its activities. Henceforth the great commission, "Go ye into all the world," became in a higher sense than even the apostles as yet understood it, the marching orders of the Church militant. And now there are signs, neither dim nor dubious, that the twentieth century will see

>Jesus enthroned where'er the sun
>Does the successive journeys run.

Let the Church universal respond: "Amen! even so come, Lord Jesus."

PAUL, APOSTLE OF THE GENTILES.

No careful student of the New Testament has failed to note what Archdeacon Farrar has styled the "dialectical method" of St. Paul as contrasted with the "intuitive method" of St. John. This difference is properly emphasized by Conybeare & Howson in their elaborate work on the "Life and Epistles of St. Paul," the Apostle of the Gentiles. It indeed may be said that even a casual reading of St. Paul's Epistles will suffice to show that he was thoroughly argumentative in his intellectual trend, leaving us to infer that the school at Tarsus was not less affected by the methods of Aristotle than was the Alexandrian philosophy by the impress of Plato, the foremost pupil of the illustrious Socrates. The Apostle's later training at the feet of Gamaliel, "the glory of the law," did not efface these marks of Greek culture. So far indeed is this from the exact truth that Paul's speech before Agrippa might have been delivered by Demosthenes in the Pnyx at Athens, and

his address on Mars' Hill was worthy of Eschines, who was only inferior to that great rival whose oratory
> Fulmined over Greece
> To Macedon and Artaxerxes' throne.

One of the Fathers has said that "if Stephen had not prayed Paul would not have preached." This is clearly an unwarrantable limitation of Divine Providence and gospel grace. God, in the accomplishment of His purposes, is not shut up by Procrustean methods or measurements. Nor does it matter in the least whether Paul's notable conversion was due to the prayer of Stephen or the thunderbolt that smote him in the way to Damascus. Whatever the cause, the contrast was none the less striking between the hot-blooded Sanhedrimist demanding *Lettres de Cachet* to Damascus and the Brother Saul who, afterward, at the bidding of Ananias, rose up and was baptized in the name of the Lord Jesus. We have always regarded this conversion of St. Paul as next to the resurrection of Christ—the strongest of the Christian evidences. I have long ceased to wonder that Lord Lyttelton, a jurist of much celebrity, was himself converted by the patient and honest investigation of this "strange and eventful history." Nor do we wonder that the Apostle made it the text and the argument of his mightiest appeals to Jew and Gentile. The miracles concerning which Hume made such a persistent pother were polemical, and, while they served an admirable purpose, they were of necessity local in their sphere and transitory in their influence. Not so with the conversion of St. Paul, an event of world-wide significance

Nor did that event fail to impress alike the first and all succeeding generations of religious thinkers. Viewed in the light of subsequent developments, it was indeed a pivotal event in the future history of the Church.

In an age of controversy, when Jew and Greek were to be confronted and confounded, not by a philosophy, but by the foolishness of preaching, it was fortunate that St. Paul was the "chosen vessel" to accomplish these great purposes. This matter of preaching was not altogether a new departure. Ezra, the Scribe, soon after the return of Israel from their captivity, had his pulpit whence he hurled "the thunder of the violated law." John the Baptist crying in the wilderness, and Peter lifting up his voice at Pentecost, had demonstrated that there was an energy in the spoken word vastly transcending the power of the written word.

But the time had arrived when the field of apostolic labor must be enlarged. Not otherwise could the kingdoms of this world become the kingdoms of our Lord and His Christ. St. Paul was quick to perceive the necessity, and accordingly his circuit was extended from Jerusalem round about unto Illyricum. Afterward, if we may trust well-authenticated tradition, he pressed westward and northward until he passed the pillars of Hercules and planted Christianity in Britain, the *ultima thule* of ancient geography. Why, indeed, might not an apostle, thoroughly alive to the claims of the gospel, follow, for the sake of souls, wherever a Phenician navigator had gone in quest of tin and copper. And this leads us quite naturally to speak of Paul as a preacher.

We have always found it somewhat difficult to reconcile the scriptural account of his evangelistic successes at Ephesus, Corinth, Thessalonica, and other chief cities with the criticism of his enemies that his bodily presence was weak and his speech contemptible. Much has been said of sundry physical ailments of the great Apostle. Sometimes it is stated that he suffered with ophthalmia or other eye disease, brought on by exposure to the intense light and heat of a Syrian sea. Others speak of his liability to epileptic seizures, as were Mohammed and Bonaparte. This is given as a reason why Luke, the beloved physician, was his frequent traveling companion. Whether there is more than a coloring of truth in these statements is fairly questionable. His long and frequent journeyings by land and sea, his exposure to and endurance of perils and hardships in city and wilderness, all are clearly incompatible with the idea that he was a physical wreck, or even a constitutional invalid. There is a moral certainty that, like Zaccheus, he was small of stature, and that for this reason he exchanged the name of Saul, suggestive of precocity—for that of Paul, which signifies little. But Palmerston, we know, was under the regulation size, and so was Douglas, of Illinois ; nor can you in any age of the world measure true manhood with a yardstick. But all this concerns only the outward man which perisheth —intellectually he was the grandest of men, and as a moral force scarcely equaled in the annals of the race.

It is noteworthy that Paul, who kept the clothes of those who slew Stephen, should have caught no little of the manner and the matter also of the protomartyr. St. Paul's defense before the great council at Jerusalem bears a striking resemblance to Stephen's defense before the same august tribunal. There is the same wealth of illustration drawn from the Jewish Scriptures, the same mighty appeal, enforced by a like impetuous oratory. Paul never at any time dallied or drawled. As has been said of Luther, and also of honest Hugh Latimer, his very words were "half-battles," or rather they might be likened to ponderous stones hurled from an ancient catapult. There was in his speech the utter absence of that flippancy that pleases "itching ears," but instead directness and impressiveness which roused and thrilled like a trumpet. I have been told that Mr. Calhoun was heard to say on more than one occasion that the great Apostle was at times an inconclusive reasoner. We see no proof of this either in his epistles or sermons. Least of all do we find it in his masterly discourse on the resurrection of the dead, which Strauss thought was open to a like adverse criticism. This German neologist refers particularly to the Apostle's reply to the question, "How are the dead raised up, and with what body do they come?" "Thou fool," says St. Paul, "that which thou sowest is not quickened except it die." Whereupon Strauss alleges that the very opposite of this statement is true, and proceeds to twit the Apostle with his utter ignorance of vegetable physiology. What solemn trifling is here, when we keep in mind that Paul employs this striking analogy not in its technical sense, but according to popular usage. What astronomer (Newton or Herschel) does not speak of the sun rising and setting, according to the vernacular of the multitude, although even Strauss would not venture to suggest that either was ignorant of the fact that the sun was stationary.

But no better vindication of the Apostle's great argument could be devised than the fact that it has withstood, like a massive sea-wall, the flood of infidel cavil and criticism that has beaten against it throughout the Christian centuries. In spite of these assaults, its defiant challenge: "O death, where is thy sting? O grave, where is thy victory?" has been the strength and stay of the dying Christian as he walked unhurt and undismayed through the valley of the shadow of death.

Take that other great argument on justification in the Epistle to the Romans, and where will you find the record of its refutation? It was the key-note of that Reformation that shook Europe from the Orkneys to Calabria. Even in this age of "higher criticism," and also of the projected revision of creeds, few men of note will be found to attack the Apostle's postulate: "Therefore, being justified by faith, we have peace with God through our Lord Jesus Christ."

We know very well that from the first century to the present time St. Paul has been charged with corrupting Christianity Late infidel writers allege that he laid undue stress on dogma, and that the controversial tone that pervades the epistles has obscured the milder spiritual effulgence of the Fourth Gospel, and almost hidden from view the ethics of the Sermon on the

Mount. We are not unduly wedded to dogmatic theology; yet, without proper emphasis of Christian doctrine, our ministry and membership are sure to drift into Broad-churchism. What would become of Geometry without its axioms and definitions? And what would be the fate of Christianity without such rigorous statement of these much-abused and much-dreaded *dogmata* as St. Paul has made prominent in his greater epistles?

There is yet a more inviting aspect of St. Paul's character, which will amply repay our consideration. We refer to his religious characteristics These best appear in his Epistle to the Philippians. Between him and the saints at Philippi there existed a closer bond of sympathy than with any of the apostolic churches. In this epistle we note especially his humility—as when he says, "I count not myself to have apprehended;" nor does he reckon himself as "already perfect." There is here no morbid self-depreciation, but such humility as is befitting the chiefest of the apostles Indeed it is only the wise man who best knows the limitations of human knowledge. So it is likewise the genuinely good man who is most conscious of the limitations of human goodness. Even in his maturity of wisdom and saintliness he is "reaching forth," and still with undiminished ardor and unstinted effort "pressing toward the mark for the prize of the high calling." How this humility, only in a measure less than the meekness of Christ, is fitted to "chasten ever lofty imagination," and even "pour contempt on all our pride!" As John Newton was humbled to the very dust when he thought of himself as once the "old African slave-trader," so Paul was deeply humiliated when he recalled the former days in which he had roamed like an evening wolf, and breathed out threatenings and slaughter against the disciples of the Lord Jesus.

But there is still another feature of his character which Mr Fletcher brings out in his "Portrait of St. Paul." We refer to his gentleness. Read his Epistle to Philemon, wherein he pleads so piteously for Onesmius, the fugitive slave, whom he had "begotten in his bonds." Study that scene by the sea-side at Miletus, and ponder well his tender leave-taking of the elders of Ephesus. If you had for a single instant supposed that St. Paul was an austere and unsympathetic man, revise your estimate while you read the pastoral letter to Timothy, his "son in the gospel," and to Titus, the first Bishop of Crete.

There remains another feature of St. Paul's character which we must not overlook, if we would have a clearcut conception of this great apostle. With all his humility and tenderness there was a courage that never faltered in any extremity of his eventful career. Stoned and dragged forth for dead at the gate of Lystra, fighting with wild beasts in the arena at Ephesus, tossed for three consecutive days on Adria, wrestling with infuriated mobs at divers times and places—never on any occasion did he so much as lose his self-possession. But never was this moral courage more severely tested than at his second and final hearing before Nero. Forsaken by friends, but strengthened by the Lord, he bore himself not less grandly than Luther at the Diet of Worms. But what of his last hours, as he was shut up alone amidst the stench and darkness and every other conceivable discomfort of a Roman prison? His second Epistle to Timothy is supposed to have been written from this confinement. Perhaps those last words, "I am now ready to be offered," etc., were written by a dim rush-light furnished him by his jailer. What trust, what resignation, what hope breathes through these words: "I have fought a good fight; I have kept the faith. Henceforth there is a crown of righteousness (brighter and better than any earthly diadem) laid up for me and for all that love His appearing!"

Here we let the curtain fall. No need to follow him to the place of doom and death on the historic Appian Way. "No prophet," said Jesus, "can perish out of Jerusalem." But an apostle, the greatest of them all, went through the city gates, bearing his cross as did the Master. Swordsman, do thy work well, and do it quickly. For, lo!

> Cherubic legions are ready to guard him home
> And shout him welcome to the skies.

O, thou tent-maker of Tarsus! thou wast indeed a valiant worker in the vineyard; and now, while the bells ring glad pæans from every turret and tower of the golden city, "enter thou into the joy of thy Lord."

An Hour's Talk With a Sea Captain.

When the gallant 10,000 that followed the standard of Xenophon in his Cyrus expedition caught their first glimpse of the ocean they shouted, "The sea! The sea!" with unspeakable rapture. It was only a less degree of joyousness that I felt when, from the deck of an ocean steamer, I got my first distinct view of the broad and billowy Atlantic. I had read books of voyages by the score before ever I had known the need of a razor. Marryat and Cooper were favorite novelists with me in my boyhood. I still retain a lively remembrance of Long Tom Coffin, the typical boatswain, and of the striking adventures of the Red Rover. Not unfrequently I dreamed at nights of the "vasty deep," ploughed by those mighty ships that "weave the continents together." Such, indeed, was my boyish enthusiasm that I have often thought that if I had been reared at a seaport, I might have started in life as a stowaway, and not as a beardless student of Blackstone.

I gravely question if Byron was ever conscious of a greater yearning "to lay his hand upon old ocean's mane and ever wanton with its breakers," and yet, after all, I was the veriest lubber in a half dozen States.

I had reached my majority before I had ever snuffed the salt sea gale, or glimpsed at a single brood of Mother Carey's chickens.

During my first and only storm at sea I fully realized my utter unfitness for a sea-faring life. How I longed for a foothold on terra firma. As I lay in my berth at midnight, and heard the stout ship struggling with a heavy sea, and felt her quiver from stem to stern, I recalled with vividness the ode of Horace, in which he berates the folly of the man who first tempted the "treacherous sea." But somehow I still have a fancy for the legends of the forecastle, and have never lost interest in the marvels and mysteries of the deep sea. Men that have gone down "to the sea in ships" still have a hold on my sympathy and veneration, and none more so than Captain J. McIntosh Kell, our present efficient Adjutant-General. Look at him with his broad, Scotch face, and his reddish hair, which betoken a "vera brither" of Rob Roy or some better highland chieftain.

It was he that fought the Alabama against the Kearsarge off the French port of Cherbourg. A wooden ship against an ironclad—the latter having the heavier battery and a larger crew. The contest was as unequal as if a light-weight pugilist should enter the ring with his bare knuckles to exchange blows with a heavy-weight with a mailed hand.

"How did it happen," I inquired of Captain Kell, a few days ago, "that you sailed out of port to fight against such odds?"

"Well," he replied, "you must remember that we could not have remained much longer in Cherbourg without going into dock. This would have demoralized and probably dispersed our crew, and thus greatly embarrassed us in all our future efforts to cripple the commerce of the enemy. Another consideration which was not without weight, was that the alternative offered us was either to fight the Kearsarge singly, or to delay and fight her and such reinforcements as she was sure to receive in a few days. But, besides, we did not know that she was an armored ship until Admiral Semmes, who was in the rigging, noticed that neither our shells nor our solid shot made any impression, but fell off into the water. We did, it is true, plant a hundred-pound shell in her stern-post, and but for a defective fuse, that single shot might have disabled our enemy or sent her to the bottom. Once into the fight, we must needs make the best possible of a bad situation."

"Did they fire on you, Captain, after you had hauled down your colors?"

"Most assuredly; they poured several broadsides into the Alabama after we had surrendered. A number of our gallant seamen were killed and wounded by this murderous fire."

"When it became evident that the Alabama was sinking, did they make an honest effort to save your men who had leaped overboard?"

"By no means. They did pick up a few, but the loss of life would have been much greater if it had not been for the magnanimous conduct of the English yacht, the Deerhound, which had come out of Cherbourg to witness the engagement.

"Mr. Seward demanded of the English Government the extradition of the rescued officers and crew, but Lord John Russell met the demand with a prompt refusal.

"Distinguished officers of the British army and navy presented Admiral Semmes with a splendid sword as some compensation for the loss of the one that went down with the Alabama."

After a breathing spell, I said to Captain Kell: "What and where was your roughest experience with storms?"

The veteran thought a moment and answered:

"The worst storm I ever encountered was off the banks of Newfoundland, where the Yankees and the Kanucks catch cod. In the East it would have been called a typhoon. It belonged to the same class of rotary storms that are named tornadoes, cyclones, etc., in different parts of the world. This one held us in its grasp for six or seven hours, and beat and battered us most unmercifully. It so happened, however, that the center or vortex of the storm passed over us, and then we were suddenly becalmed. When in this vortex the mercury in the barometer, which just before the storm had sunk nearly to twenty-eight inches, immediately began to rise. During this lull Admiral Semmes ordered a storm sail to be set, as we knew we would catch the storm in a few minutes from the opposite quarter. It would be impossible to convey an adequate idea of the fury of this terrible typhoon. Our main-yard was snapped like a pipestem and our sails were rent into ribbons.

"We estimated that this vast revolving atmospheric cylinder had a radius of about fifty miles. Eolus, or the satan of the book of Job, or whoever else is 'the prince of the powers of the air,' fairly churned the sea into a blinding and almost stifling spray."

"I find," said I to the Captain, "that in Semmes' volume, 'Memoirs of Service Afloat,' you were once court-martialed for mutiny and disobedience to orders."

"Thereby," said our interlocutor, "hangs a tale. At the time referred to I held the rank of passed midshipman on the war sloop Albany, Captain Victor Randolph, of Virginia, commanding. Lieutenant Randolph ordered me, in a rather peremptory manner, to light a candle and carry it to the cabin. Now, you must remember, that I was not only, as a youngster would be, a little proud of my rank, but I had in my veins also a little of the rebel blood that made my ancestors, the McIntoshes, fight against the house of Hanover at Preston Pans and Culloden. The military disaster that followed the latter event led some of them to come to Darien, in this State, shortly before our revolutionary troubles began. I refused to obey the Lieutenant's order because I esteemed it a menial service. In spite, however, of Lieutenant Raphael Semmes' able defense of me before the court-martial, I was dismissed from the navy. A year afterwards, through the influence of Senator Berrien and Mr. Toombs, I was reinstated with my former rank, with only the loss of my year's pay, which, in those days, was to me a mere bagatelle. I feel it due to myself to say that I had the full sympathy of my brother passed midshipmen, and, indeed, most of the officers and all the crew."

"I think, Captain," I continued, " that you took part in the capture of California during the Mexican war."

"Yes," he rejoined, "I was a Lieutenant on board the frigate Savannah, the flagship of Commodore Slote, of the Pacific squadron. We landed at Monterey and in a solemn manner unfurled the American flag, and by this imposing ceremony took possession of the country. This, in the parlance of the lawyers, was a kind of wholesale livery of seizin. Of course the affair would have been farcical, but for the fact, that we were backed by the whole power, military and naval, of the government."

"Were you not," we asked, "with Commodore Perry when he negotiated the first treaty of commerce with the Japanese?"

"Yes," he replied, "I was on board of the Susquehanna, one of the best ships of our East India squadron. It was an historical occasion, when we landed over 1,000 marines on the coast of Jeddo, one of the largest islands of the Japanese group. Hard by, with heavy guns bearing on the island, was our fleet, composed of seven of the best ships of the old navy. In a unique building, elevated for the purpose, Commodore Perry, with his staff, met the representatives of the Tycoon—the brother of the sun, the first cousin of the moon, and the near kinsman of innumerable stars, with a few comets thrown in for good measure. There was about that affair but little of the red-tapism of Downing street. Our gallant Perry being a plain, blunt man, with an eye for business, it did not require much diplomatic palaver to break the seal of seclusion that had for so long a time isolated Japan from western civilization. The little Dutch trading port at Nagasaki was lost sight of, and the best ports of the empire were henceforth open to American commerce.

"We begin now to reap the reward of that naval enterprise in the vast increase of commercial exchanges, and in the rapid growth of Christianity in a country where, a half century ago, children were taught to trample on the cross, the despised symbol of the Christian faith."

"What about the superstitions of the sailor and the crossing of the line, concerning which we formerly read so much in the old story books of the nursery?"

"Well," replied the Captain, "these are passing away as the years go by. Old Neptune, armed with his trident, rarely comes up the ship's side as in former times, to the consternation of the fresh water sailors and the younger middies. The average sailor, however, has not yet overcome his aversion to leaving port on Friday, nor his dislike to carrying a dead body on shipboard."

"What have you to say about the qualities of the American sailor?"

"Only this—that the thoroughbred downeaster is the best seaman that sails the ocean. He is handy and trusty, and has little dread of storms or shells. Next to him, and in special directions superior to him, is the British tar, who followed Nelson and Collingwood in their great ocean victories. Comparatively few sailors are of Southern birth or blood, but some of the best men on the Sumter and Alabama were shipped at Charleston and Savannah. Not a few of the best naval officers in the Yankee service during the late war were Southern men. Of these we name Farragut and Hewitt. Indeed, the great body of our Southern born naval officers, from Maryland to Texas, followed the leadership of Hollins and Raphael Semmes, and that 'old sea dog,' Tatnall, who cast their lot with their native Southland. The record they made with the Merrimac, the Sumter, the Shenandoah, and, above all, with the peerless and ill-fated Alabama, is one of which their countrymen need not be ashamed."

But the noble old sea-fighter must hurry off to Sunnyside, where his noble wife and only son, the future admiral, await his coming.

At the risk of incurring Captain Kell's displeasure we reproduce, without his knowledge, a letter from his old commander addressed to his godson, the little boy already referred to in the foregoing sentence. It presents Admiral Semmes in a new role, and shows that a great man may have on occasion the simplicity and gentleness of a little child:

MOBILE, ALA., May 6, 1870.

MY DEAR LITTLE GODSON :—I have received your little letter, together with your likeness. You have grown to be quite a little man since I saw you. You are no doubt acquiring to learn to spell, and by-and-by you will be a "big boy" and go to school. I am sorry to hear that your papa is not very well. Tell mamma to take good care of him. In the meantime you must be a good little boy and do all papa and mamma tell you, so that you may grow up to be a man like your papa.

     Your affectionate godfather,
             R. SEMMES.

Paragraphic Pencilings.

Paragraphic Pencilings.

The telescope was the first optical instrument to familiarize us with the vastness of the universe. In the presence of such immense distances and incomprehensible magnitudes as it reveals we stand awe-struck and almost paralyzed. But a later invention, the microscope, has brought within the range of human vision a countless multitude of vegetable and animal organisms that overwhelm us by their minuteness.

A solitary blade of grass is the abode of a vast bacterial population, and a single raindrop from a summer cloud has stored up in it the potencies of a thunder storm. A small cake of yeast will develop millions of fermentative cells, nor would there be any assignable limit to their reproduction, were it not arrested by the heat of the baker's oven. These infinitesimal forces are at work everywhere. Those tiny insects, the corals, that build up continents and islands from such depths as the plummet of the Challenger never reached, are of mammoth-like proportions compared with the bacilli which wield such an influence on human health and happiness.

This remark brings us face to face with the greatest medical discovery since the days of Edward Jenner. Of course, we refer to Dr. Koch's discovery of the bacillus which produces lupus, tuberculosis and kindred diseases. It has been achieved in spite of criticism and personal discomfort Not only has it been sneered at by the *profanum vulgus*, but by jealous scientists, and yet it will solve important problems and both promote health and prolong life. As yet the treatment is in its infancy, but coming generations will honor the memory of that illustrious German, who at one time expatriated himself and at another immured himself in the laboratory that he might prosecute his researches. Thus one by one the storehouse of nature is yielding its precious secrets, and this widening of the domain of knowledge will go forward for centuries. Who can measure the results of the recent exploration of the dark continent? Hitherto its material products have been chiefly gold and ivory. But now that the higher races have undertaken its development, we may look for marvelous discoveries that may make it the richest, as it is the oldest, of the five great continents. Here we might call a halt, and still we have said nothing of electricity, that Ariel of the chemist's laboratory. What strides it has made since Franklin was flying his kite over Boston Common! Already it seems destined to supplant steam as a motor. Even now it lights our streets and dwellings, and very soon will warm our bedchambers and cook our meals. It has revolutionized, in a degree, some of the useful arts, and is stretching forth its Briarean hands to new conquests in other industrial fields. Only that Omniscient Eye that sees the end from the beginning can forecast the possibilities of its future.

At one period of his life, David, the valiant son of Jesse, was not less an outlaw than Robin Hood, of Sherwood Forest. For months he was hunted like a partridge on the mountains by Saul and his soldiery. But he was reserved to a kingly destiny and became the Napoleon of his age.

It was in the earlier days of his eventful life that an incident occurred which gives us a glimpse of his nobility of character. On one occasion he was seized with a passionate longing for a drink of water from the well of Bethlehem, then garrisoned by the Philistines. He spoke of this yearning, and, without waiting to be bidden, three of his bravest liegemen—possibly the sons of Zeruiah—broke through the Philistine array and fetched him the coveted draught.

David, realizing that it had been obtained at the peril of the lives of these gallant men, refused the draught and poured it out as a kind of drink-offering to the Lord.

This was but one of the many striking displays of his magnanimity. But his life was marred by some grievous faults, which he laments in the seven penitential psalms. For some of these pronounced transgressions he was sorely punished by the insubordination of Joab, the bad faith of his trusted counselor, Ahithophel, and the rebellion and death of Absalom, his favorite son and the heir of his throne. How true the saying of William Jay, the prince of preachers, that "the best of men are but men at the best." Abraham's dissimulation, Noah's drunkenness, Jacob's sharp practice, Solomon's lechery, and so on to the end of the chapter. The perfect candor of the writers of these historical books of the Old Testament utterly refutes the infidel notion that they were in any sense pious frauds. And how do these sacred biographies, and profane history as well, teach us that the grandest men of universal history fall infinitely below Jesus of Nazareth, who after the flesh was both the root and the offspring of David, but who likewise in no dubious sense was the "'only begotten of the Father, full of grace and truth!"

Of late years very much stress has been laid on the law of heredity, but recently Professor Weismann, of Germany, has made a vigorous fight against the transmission of culture from parent to offspring. Some leading scientists, amongst them Alfred Russell Wallace, have indorsed his views, and the contest will be sharp, if not decisive. The probability is that after a period of disputation a compromise will be reached. What is known as ativism is measurably true both in anatomy and psychology, but the exceptions are so many and the intervals are so wide that the law is of little practical benefit. Some diseases, notably phthisis and insanity, are now regarded as of doubtful transmissibility. At least it is not so much the disease itself that is transmitted as certain susceptibilities to the disease. The uniform tendency in nature is to repair injuries of every sort and thus to prevent their recurrence in offspring.

It was John Randolph, I believe, who said that moral monsters could not propagate. The same conservatism holds in regard to physical degeneracy. "Margaret, the gutter-snipe," was no less exceptional in the matter of motherhood than are the parents of double-headed calves or three-legged chickens. Whether we admit or deny a Divine Providence in these and other matters, there is a uniformity of sequence in the processes of the universe that denote both a law and a law-giver.

These facts which are being brought to the front by scientific research are worth all the metaphysics of the Bridgewater treatises and of the Bampton lectures.

John Wesley is reported to have said that if he died worth more than enough to pay his debts and funeral expenses, he wanted to be considered a thief and a robber. These may not be his exact words, but this is the substance of several of his deliverances. This great man was equally averse to the increase of wealth amongst the Methodist people. He forewarned them that affluence would bring luxury and its attendant irregularities. In this way the church would lose its spirituality and its hold on the masses. As a preventive, he resolved for himself to make all he could and give all he could, and enjoined the same line of policy on his people. Mr. Wesley, however, lived to see a vast change in the social and financial condition of his followers. The sixty dollar salary of Bishop Asbury has grown to some thousands, and there are now on the American continent single Methodist churches that pay more money than the old Georgia Conference did in the early days of the Pierces and

Arnold and Hull and others of the fathers. Has the spiritual decay followed the fear of which disquieted the mind of the immortal founder? We might answer both yes and no. There is, nowadays, less of the hallelujah feature—the amen corner, when not wholly deserted, responds feebly to the good points of the pulpit. The general rule touching gold and costly apparel is in many quarters a nullity. There is less simplicity in Methodist worship—less closet devotion; less Bible study outside of the Sunday-schools. In some directions, however, there has been manifest improvement. The church is expending large sums, compared with other periods of its history; immense amounts indeed for church literature, home and foreign missions, church building and extension and current church expenses. Now, as aforetime, there are drones that neither pay nor pray. There is room for improvement in both directions, especially in the latter. After all, Methodism has been a grand religious movement. Despite the shortcomings of its ministry and membership, it has not been a whit behind its older sister churches in evangelical piety and ecclesiastical aggressiveness. It has compassed the earth by its missionary enterprises, and whereas in its infancy it was a feeble and despised sect, worshipping in barns and groves, it now has its splendid churches, its well-endowed colleges and spacious hospitals. Thousands of the most cultured people, and, what is better, many more of the saintliest men and women worship at its altars. With its present moral and financial resources, it only needs to "walk in the old paths, wherein is the good way," and her growth before the close of the twentieth century will make her the joy of the angels and the glory of our common Christendom.

Shelley was never at any pains to conceal his atheistic sentiments. When an undergraduate at Oxford he published a pamphlet denouncing Christianity as a fraud and a failure. In after years, when he should have learned the folly of this collegiate blunder, he wrote his name on the register of the Hospice St. Gothard—Percy Bysshe Shelley, atheist. There, in the midst of the great mountains, which were striking emblems of God's majesty and righteousness, he exhibited that impiety that in his case bordered on insanity. How else could it have been that Shelley would start with seeming affright and break out into blasphemous utterances at the mentioning of the name of Jesus? I know of nothing parallel to it, except in the case of Julian, the apostate, whose dying utterance, "Oh, Galilean, thou hast conquered!" was the outcry of baffled hate and concentrated bitterness.

Few persons of this generation read much of Shelley. Indeed, except his lines "To a Skylark," and parts of his "Cenci," a tragedy, there is little of his poetry that will abide.

Early in life I was greatly enamored of Shelley, and it is possible the reaction of later years has swung the pendulum too far in the opposite direction.

Few men who meet Colonel R. F. Maddox, the banker, and first-class Atlantian, would ever infer that he was once the champion bugler of Western Georgia. When as yet he had not reached his legal majority he was the bugler of the Harris County Cavalry company. This company was composed of the solid men of those parts, and it was a treat to watch their maneuverings when on parade. Judge Crawford, of the Supreme Court, at one time commanded the company, and by his efforts brought them to a good state of drill and discipline. On review days and other special occasions, Bob Maddox rode at the head of the cavalry and played his bugle for all it was worth. He was of good stock, for his ancestry were Methodists of a school nearly extinct, except in the outlying rural districts. They belonged to that "bold peasantry" whom Goldsmith called "their country's pride," from whom are recruited our best city population. Colonel Maddox and myself often meet and talk over the old times, and both of us have pleasant memories of "old Harris" and its excellent people. Since these arcadian days we have both had our trials and successes, but we often think, and perchance dream by day and night, of Pine mountain and its picturesque views, and of the charming valleys through which murmur the beautiful streams along whose banks we fished and frolicked in boyhood.

Dr. Lafferty, of the *Richmond Advocate*, alludes to Rev. Dr. R. L. Dabney, the distinguished Presbyterian divine, as one of the giants of the century. He further commends him for a vigorous article in a late church paper on the subject of "Hell Fire Preaching." This is the sort of pulpit teaching that is greatly needed at the present day. Too many of our pulpits are converted into lecture platforms, and have consequently lost the old-time force that "turned the world upside down." Less German philosophy, with more evangelical fervor, is "mighty through God to the pulling down of strongholds." For a man "to court a smile where he should win a soul" is a species of ministerial trifling that deserves to be scouted from the temple of the Most High.

Not everybody will remember how, that many years ago, one Bullock defaulted as cashier of the Central Railroad Bank at Savannah. The offender belonged to one of the best families, and his trial and conviction produced quite an uproar in social, as well as commercial circles. His bondsmen suffered heavily, and the atmosphere of the Forest City was for quite awhile fairly lurid with curses, both loud and deep. Amongst these bondsmen were Dr. Arnold, and a Presbyterian deacon, Albert Lewis, whose behavior was sharply contrasted. The latter, in conversation with Dr. Arnold, said that the loss hurt him worse than anybody. "Why so?" asked Dr. Arnold; "my money is worth as much to me as yours is to you." "But," replied the deacon, "you get rid of your bad feelings by cursing, but I am a member of the church and am debarred from the use of that remedy." Whereupon Dr. Arnold rejoined that he was thankful that he could exercise the rights of an American democrat, without let or hindrance. It is well known that an explosion of expletives, even of a wicked sort, does lessen the nervous tension and rid the system of its surplus bile. Nor need we go far to find the philosophy of the matter. But it is better under all provocations to obey the precept of St. James, "Swear not at all."

"Before and after taking" is a favorite illustration of the patent medicine vendor. In these crude etchings the difference between the physical appearance of the same man at two periods of his life are exaggerated for purposes of gain. "Before taking" he looks as though he had just escaped from a cemetery, minus the grave clothes. "After taking" he seems robust and ready for the prize ring. This difference is not more striking than between the popular estimate of some poets, living and dead. Only the other day an appreciative New Yorker endowed the cottage at Fordham, which was for some years occupied by Edgar Allan Poe, with the handsome sum of $50,000, the cottage to be held and perpetuated as a memorial of our greatest American poet. It was there that the girl-wife, variously called the "lost Lenore," the "beautiful Anabel Lee," so beautiful indeed that even "the angels envied her favored lover, "the saintly Ulalume," was buried in

> The ghoul-haunted woodland of Weir.

It was there, we repeat, she sickened and died in the

arms of her frantic lover. It was there also that Poe, half crazed with grief in that bleak December night, wrought out that marvelous poem, "The Raven." For that work he received from the *American* (whig) *Review* the beggarly sum of $10, the weekly wages of a vulgar hireling. What recks the dead literary demigod, as he lies now in his neglected grave at Baltimore, of these post-mortem honors? Verily we Americans are also given to stoning the prophets, and as some amends to their outraged majesty we garnish their sepulchres.

Gladstone seems to have a standing quarrel with Professor Huxley. Its long continuance gives to this warfare of words the appearance of a theological vendetta. The last phase of it relates to the "swine miracle" in the coasts of Gadara. The great English leader insists that the scriptural narrative of the healing of the demoniac who had his dwelling amongst the tombs, and of the subsequent fate of the herd of swine, is sober history. Professor Huxley argues that the whole transaction is mythical, and therefore entitled to no credit.

It is fortunate for the Christian system that its pillars do not rest on these surface facts. The whole of these might be swept into oblivion, and yet not one jot or tittle of its essential truth would be affected thereby. If, in the intervals of official engagements, Gladstone can find time to try conclusions with the scientists on these side issues, it may be well; but, with due deference to the learned combatants, we seriously question "if the game is worth the candle."

The thought of the world, like its civilization, moves in a circle; therefore it is that history repeats itself. Even in this age of iron we are now and then confronted with curious speculations as to apparitions, witchcraft, clairvoyance, and other phases of what the French call "diablerie." After all the flippant talk about human progress, the most advanced races have not fully outgrown the love of such studies, nor the belief in their alleged facts. Only the other night, in conversation with my wife, I heard quite distinctly the keys of the piano trill for a single instant in the front room. No one else was in the house, and in reason's spite I was conscious of a nervous twitching. After a moment's reflection, I mentally exclaimed, "Rats!" and dismissed the subject. Perhaps I had struck the proper solution; possibly was wide of the mark. After all, it may have been a sensory illusion. I suppose there is hardly a well regulated household that has not its traditional ghost story. At the risk of being thought egotistic, I will tell one in my father's family.

In 1846, my brother, Andrew D. Scott, then a resident of Columbus, enlisted in Company A, of the first regiment of Georgia Volunteers that went to Mexico. The latest communication received from him was written at Camargo, on the Rio Grande, just as he was leaving with his regiment for Monterey. Several weeks elapsed before we had further tidings of him. During this interval, we naturally became quite anxious about him. This was especially true of my father, whose health at the time was much impaired. On the night of the 13th of December, 1846, my father waked my mother and said to her: "Wife, I have had a very unpleasant dream about Andrew. It was so vivid that I fear it has some significance. I dreamed that he came into this room and stood just here by the bed. He was looking like himself, except that he was pale and had a sorrowful expression of countenance. I said to him: 'Son, how is it you are here?' He replied: 'Father, I am dead.'" My mother rallied him gently on his nervousness, assuring him that there was nothing in a dream. About ten days thereafter my father received a letter from Captain Calhoun, of Company A, stating that the regiment had been ordered from Monterey to Tampico, and that my brother and his old schoolmate, Fleming G. Davies, of Milledgeville, had been left seriously ill in a hospital at Monterey. Some weeks thereafter, we had a letter from Mark H. Blandford, of the same regiment, lately a judge of the Supreme Court, informing us that he had understood that this brother died on the night of the 13th of December, at Monterey, and was buried, his grave being marked for future identification. The dream and the death we were then, and now are, satisfied occurred on the same night. Of course we believed there was no ghostly visitation, that the whole affair was subjective, and the coincidence purely fortuitous. A large number of very similar instances are recorded in books of science, notably by Abercrombie and Upham. Quite recently we have seen the statement from an able writer that ghosts "are neither flesh and blood entities, nor extremely tenuous bodies, but the result of the telepathic action of one mind on another."

This definition reminds us of Huxley's definition of evolution. Both need some one to interpret them to the laity.

Sir Walter Scott was wont to liken James I. of England to an old gander running about and cackling all manner of nonsense. The provocation must have been very great that would have induced the author of "Waverly" to speak thus irreverently of a crowned head, especially of a Stuart. But James deserved this and more, for he was a first-class nuisance in court and country. This royal pupil of George Buchanan had a profound conviction that he had mastered the science of kingcraft, and therefore he was continually seeking to thrust his views about all sorts of things, great or small, upon his subjects.

He had a childish dread of witches and an invincible dislike to heretics, two of whom he caused to be burned at Smithfield. When Sir Walter Raleigh introduced tobacco into the realm he turned author and wrote a most furious and pedantic "Counterblast" against its use. When his Queen Anne of Denmark imported the farthingale from France he issued a royal proclamation against this style of female underwear. He was not without learning of a sort, but his lack of practical sense made him a perpetual bore when he was not a laughing stock in his own palace. Possibly, if he had been a wiser sovereign, Raleigh would not have been beheaded nor Bacon disgraced. He transmitted to his son and successor a zeal for Episcopacy and prerogative that cost him his throne and cost England twenty-five years of civil war.

There is no solitude like that which may be found in a great city. When Cowper was heartsick and weary of the garrulity of Mrs. Unwin and her tea drinking neighbors, he wished for "a lodge in some vast wilderness." The poet of "The Task" would have found quicker relief if he had plunged into the heart of London. What a man, in his nervous condition, needs is diversion quite as much as seclusion. But if the latter is desired it can be better secured in a great metropolis than in "some boundless contiguity of shade." It is related of Dr. Johnson that for forty years he walked through the streets of London, when, by the merest chance, he met the first time a schoolboy friend who had come to that vast city the same year and month with himself. Although their residences were only a few squares apart, yet during that long period, their paths never crossed.

Who was the "War Horse of Troup?" We put this question a few days ago to a lady who was reared in LaGrange. She promptly and rather naively answered: "I suppose Governor Gordon or Burrus Jones." Both these gentlemen were rather conspicuous for their fighting qualities during the late war. Some queer things are told of Colonel Jones, especially his coolness under fire. It is said that when on picket duty with his regiment, his habit (whenever the enemy's fire slackened) was to light his pipe and sit down to his favorite game of "Old Sledge." But the real war horse of Troup was Colonel Julius C. Alford, of whom current literature makes but little mention. During the Creek and Seminole troubles he made an enviable reputation as a soldier, but with the details of his military career we are in no wise familiar. In the presidential campaign of 1840 he was known far and wide as the "War Horse of Troup." Indeed, he was a man of stalwart build, a ready debater, and of a personal courage that never flickered in any presence. He was one of the few Whig campaigners that could measure swords with Walter T. Colquitt. They were well matched on the hustings, for Colquitt, although of less physical power, had equal or superior gifts as an orator, and a like faculty for enthusing his audience. To compare things strikingly unlike, we might say they were as well matched as Bill Stallings and Bob Durham, the respective bullies of the upper and lower battalions, whom Longstreet has so vividly portrayed in "Georgia Scenes." The issue of the fight which Longstreet describes, settled the championship of the country as between Stallings and Durham, the latter wearing the belt. The Whigs and Democrats, however, could never agree as to whether Alford or Colquitt was the champion debater. The only time I ever heard Alford was at an immense barbecue held in the High School grove at LaGrange. Dr. R. A. T. Ridley presided and introduced the speakers. Besides Colonel

Alford, I remember Colonel Hutchinson, of Montgomery, Ala., who was quaintly surnamed the "Prairie Bull." His boisterous delivery may have suggested this ungainly sobriquet. He afterwards entered the Methodist ministry, and died, I believe, a distinguished member of the Alabama conference. Colonel Alford, who was on his native heath, came last, and, by his severe castigation of the Van Buren administration, and his decidedly emphatic way of stating his facts and figures about extravagance in the White House, he fully entitled himself to be called the "War Horse of Troup." To speak more soberly, Colonel Alford was a man of marked ability, who attained to legislative and congressional honors. But for a comparatively early death, he would have reached yet higher distinction in the councils of the nation. Some of his descendants and other relatives are amongst the best people of Troup and adjoining counties.

Peter the Great well deserves to be styled what a late writer has called "a beacon light of history." Nor is another historian wide of the mark when he describes him as an "inspired barbarian." Be that as it may, he was in a better sense the founder of that immense military power, which now overshadows both northern Europe and Asia, than was the Great Frederick, the founder of the vast German Empire. When Peter came to the throne his people were, indeed, in a semi-barbarous condition. The story of his travels in disguise through Europe, observing the civilizations that he was anxious to introduce into his own Muscovite realm, reads like a romance—especially the statement that for months he worked in the dock-yards of Holland that he might master the craft of shipbuilding. But as yet Russia had no outlet to the great oceans of the world, and it was to accomplish that purpose that Peter built a new capital, St. Petersburg, in the marshes of the Neva, hoping to effect his object through the gulf of Finland and the Baltic sea. Later sovereigns of the house of Romanoff have steadfastly pursued the same policy. But for the last half century and more they have aimed at the seizure of Constantinople and egress by the Bosphorus into the Mediterranean, on whose shores have flourished and fallen some of the greatest civilizations of the world's history.

Since the days of Catherine II., the legend, "This is the way to Constantinople," has been the keynote to Russian progress and the inspiration of military aggressiveness. Indeed this is the gist of the eastern question that has so often disturbed the midnight slumbers of Downing street and sorely perplexed the diplomacy of Paris and Berlin.

Nor was this question definitely settled by the charge at Balaklava or the storming of the Redan. England has not relaxed her grip on the Sultan, nor has the Czar ceased to covet the Danubian principalities, and along with these Constantinople, the last foothold of Islamism on the European continent. This is to-day the greatest living issue of European politics. It is greater by far than the Alsace and Lorraine issue;

greater than the Egyptian embroglio and a more urgent issue than whether Germany or England shall control on the banks of the Congo. There is a strange vitality in this eastern question, as we have defined it. It recalls the emphatic utterances of the elder Cato, "*Delerda est Carthago,*" with which he closed every address to the Roman Senate. The utterance was prophetic and Carthage received her death-blow at the hands of Scipio Africanus on the plains of Zama. Sooner or later likewise the Czar of all the Russias will ride in triumph through the streets of Constantine's favorite capitol. Less than six months before the untimely and lamented death of Henry Grady, he asked me when and where would be fought the battle of Gog and Magog. I answered that the usual opinion was that this last conflict would be waged on the plains of Esdraelon the Flanders of Hebrew history. But that another opinion was that this decisive struggle would take place under the walls of Constantinople, where Christian and Saracen had so often and so stoutly contended for the mastery. In his speech at the University of Virginia a few days thereafter, (which was his best literary work), he made some brilliant points on this Armageddon affair.

I once heard a minister of high rank preach on the hackneyed pulpit theme of "Family Government." There was in the discourse a goodly measure of commonplace moralizing, but there was one remark that was solid and suggestive, and that deserves to be written on the lintels of every Christian home. It was in these words: "If you would have your child love you, you must exact of him thorough obedience." This precept is as weighty as the best saying of the seven wise men of Greece. Where one child is won by parental indulgence a hundred are alienated and spoiled for life by this sort of leniency. Ancestral worship is the basis of all true religion. Fatherhood is a sacred trust, and whatever lowers its dignity or weakens its authority is a curse to the household and a damage to society. We offer no apology for the domestic tyrant who rules his family with a mailed hand or by any other law than that of kindness. Children and servants have rights which even *pater familias* is bound to respect. But to suffer them, from mistaken fondness, to grow up like the "wild ass' colt," is to do them a grievous wrong. Whether the rod is to be employed in the rearing of the child depends very much on the temperament of the child and but little less on the temper of the parent. An angry father who, in such a mood, belabors a rude boy with a hickory or a cowhide, is very sure to "provoke him to wrath," contrary to the apostolic injunction. In such cases the infliction is worse than the evil sought to be remedied. With these necessary qualifications, the maxim, "spare the rod and spoil the child," while not, as is sometimes claimed, scriptural in its literal acceptation, is, notwithstanding, in human experience not without "confirmation strong as proofs of Holy Writ."

East Tennessee loyalty reached its high water mark after the surrender of Appomatox. Of course there were honorable exceptions, but in the main the political following of Brownlow, Etheridge and Andy Johnson consisted of the riff-raff of the mountaineers, who were as thoroughly wedded to the stars and stripes as were the provincialists of La Vendee to the Bourbon dynasty in the early days of the French revolution. During the contest they were intensely bitter and proscriptive and but little esteemed even by their associates for their soldierly qualities. But when the cruel war was over they vented their spleen on the "secesh," driving out many of the best citizens and grossly abusing others, especially the preachers of the Southern Methodist church. Some of this latter class were beaten unmercifully by the loyal kuklux for no crime except the preaching of a non-political gospel. East Tennessee, as well as Missouri, had its Methodist martyrs, such as the venerable Brillhart and the saintly Neal. In 1866, I made a business tour through this section, occasionally preaching at some personal peril, as at Athens, where the Southern Methodists were excluded from their own church and compelled to worship in the court house. On Monday thereafter the town was thronged with blue coats, who were somewhat given to rowdyism Two or three times during the day I was pointed out and opprobriously designated by the coarse military rabble as the "rebel preacher."

Some of my friends were apprehensive that I might

meet with harsher treatment, but I escaped any personal violence. At Cleveland and Knoxville matters had righted up to a great extent, but even at these points the fires of hate were smouldering rather than extinguished. Rev. Dr. Park, the Presbyterian pastor at Knoxville, weathered out the storm of war and was unflinchingly faithful to the Confederate cause. He gave me much sympathy during my stay in Knoxville and much information which I cannot now recall. He still survives and enjoys the love and reverence of all good people. Here I renewed my acquaintance with that grand Methodist layman, J. W. Gaut, whom I had frequently met in Georgia during the war period. Atlanta was greatly benefited by the exodus of Southern men from East Tennessee. Moore and Marsh and Lowry and Hopkins and the Inmans, and others of Atlanta's foremost citizens were drifted Southward by the cumpulsive current of sectional animosity.

A Presbyterian friend asks me to take a hand in the pending controversy—"Shall Women be Allowed to Preach?" With the thermometer up in the nineties and still suffering with a remnant of LaGrippe, I am not in the mood for such heavy work. If the eager public will be patient the question will settle itself. Isolated texts, whether from Peter or Paul, cannot arrest the movement, especially when the texts themselves are of doubtful interpretation. Let us quietly and prayerfully await the developments of Providence. Of one thing I am quite sure, that several of the devout women that I have heard preach are quite equal in gifts and graces to the average pulpiteer of the male persuasion. All this is aside from the widely different question of licensure or ordination.

We frequently stumble on journalistic discussions of the comparative value of genius and talent. Like Macaulay, we have a hearty abhorrence of the latter term, especially the adjective, "talented." It is in sooth the characteristic of the coarser mental and moral fibre, and belongs as little to the higher realm of intellect as a sewing machine to the department of fine arts. As respects genius, it is everywhere a divine gift, and is not less inspirational than prophecy. Whether we trace its footprints in the Inferno of Dante or the transfiguration of Raphael, we stand reverent, with uncovered head and unsandalled feet, as did Moses at the burning bush, or with mouth in the dust, as when Jehovah spoke to his servant Job out of the whirlwind. We don't undervalue industry as a means of achieving greatness, but it is an indifferent substitute for the highest order of genius. These two, talent and genius, are, as a mathematician would say, incommensurable quantities. The loftiest flights of oratory, as in the case of Mirabeau and Burke the sublimest reaches of the imagination, as in Faust and the Iliad, can never be rivaled by mere talent, however deep and broad. The history of literature is replete with these ambitious efforts. It is, after all, soaring on Dedalian wings that melt in the sunlight of the Empyrean. To illustrate, Everett was a man of talent. His fellow-countryman, Webster, was a genius. And so on through the list of great names.

Two highly esteemed personal friends, Dr. R. B. Ridley and Judge George Hillyer, have mentioned to me an English review of a recent date, which is highly laudatory of our Georgia poet, Sidney Lanier. The English critic places Lanier in the front rank of American bards. Several years ago we had occasion to write and print an elaborate article on Lanier, in which we assigned him a like position. We even ventured to say that neither Alexander Pope nor John Dryden, in their tribute to music, had equaled his masterpiece, "The Symphony." The English reviewer further says that Lanier surpasses both Tennyson and Browning. This estimate needs little modification. The time is nigh at hand when this illustrious Georgian will be hailed as the greatest poet of the present generation.

How much is it to be deplored that contemporary criticism in his case was so greatly mistaken in its appreciation of him! Strange to say, there were professional reviewers that went wild over the oftentimes vapid versification of Longfellow that sought to damn Lanier with faint praise. What think some of these of the following which one of the most cultured literateurs in America pronounces a diamond of the first water?

A BALLAD OF TREES AND THE MASTER.

Into the woods my Master went
Clean forspent, forspent.
Into the woods my Master came
Forspent with love and shame.
But the olives they were not blind to Him;
The little gray leaves were kind to Him;
The thorn tree had a mind to Him,
When into the woods He came.

Out of the woods my Master came
And He was well content.
Out of the woods my Master came
Content with death and shame.
When death and shame would woo Him last;
From under the trees they drew Him last;
'Twas on a tree they slew Him last,
When out of the woods He came.

What Raphael's "Madonna" is in sacred art, this ballad is in Christian song.

The remains of the first man that I ever saw who had been slain in battle, were those of Major Ringgold, the gallant artillerist of Taylor's army. They were carried through, overland, by the old Piedmont line of stages to Baltimore. They were placed on top of the coach, while a small escort occupied the body of the coach. It will be remembered that Ringgold fell in the first regular battle of the Mexican war, May 8th, 1846, at Palo Alto, a few miles from Point Isabel. Taylor, at the head of 2,000 men, was marching to the relief of Major Brown at Matamoras. General Arista, of the Mexican army, who a few days before had surprised and captured Captain

Thornton and his dragoons, placed his army of 6,000 athwart Taylor's line of march. At Palo Alto they met, when the Mexicans were driven back to Resaca de la Palma, where a heavier engagement occurred on the 9th, which resulted in a thorough defeat of the enemy. It was in this last battle that Captain May and his dragoons charged a Mexican battery and captured General La Vega, who was in command of the battery. Ringgold and May, who were the heroes of the hour, were Southern men. The first departure of troops for the seat of war that I ever witnessed was at Milledgeville in 1835. It was a small body who went to join others at Macon and go forward to reinforce the Texans under Sam Houston. My recollection is that they narrowly missed the massacre of the Alamo and shared in the crowning victory of San Jacinto in the following April.

Charles Phillips, the eloquent Irish barrister, in emphasizing the inconsistencies of the First Napoleon, says of him, amongst other things—"a professed Catholic, he imprisoned the Pope." To understand the true import of this statement we must needs refer to the matrimonial vagaries of "the man of destiny." Most people know something of his abandonment of the beautiful and devoted Creole widow of Beauharnais, who gave him her heart and hand when as yet he was "unknown to fortune and to fame." Very few, however, are aware of the fact that this marriage was solemnized in 1796 according to revolutionary forms and not by a Catholic priest. For this reason it was regarded by Pius VII., the reigning pontiff, as uncanonical. Pius, however, recognized it as a civil contract and therefore binding in the Court of Conscience. When Napoleon afterwards, desiring for purely political reasons to put aside the wife of his youth, asked the Pope to sanction his adulterous marriage with Maria Louisa, the Hapsburg princess, the request was declined. This refusal was made at great personal risk, and really subjected him to more than a constructive imprisonment, first in Rome itself, and again at Fontainebleau. It may have been to coerce the Pope that Napoleon seized St. Peter's patrimony and annexed it to the Empire long before the time of Victor Emanuel.

Napoleon I., like Henry VIII., when he set his heart on Anne Boleyn, would listen to no ghostly counsel, but proceeded, in spite of the tears and entreaties and swoonings of Josephine, to the consummation of a marriage which allied him to one of the oldest dynasties of Europe. We need not say that the results were disappointing in more respects than one. It was a just retribution which befell him, in that, although his Austrian wife gave birth to a male heir in less than a year after her espousal, yet it was not the king of Rome, as he was boastfully called, but a grandson of Josephine, his repudiated wife, that came to the throne of the French Empire. It may seem superstitious, and yet we will venture the remark that it was this Austrian alliance that paved the way to the decline and ultimate downfall of Bonapartism. He was prompted to it by "a vaulting ambition that overleaped itself." It not only failed to conciliate the crowned heads, but it compromised his honor with the masses who had hitherto rejoiced in his good fortune. This it was that gave double fury to the winds of adversity that followed the inglorious Russian campaign. This it was that sent him an exile to Elba, and after the hundred days ending at Waterloo, shut him up a State prisoner at St. Helena.

When on that "lone, barren rock" he passed away, not with New Jerusalem visions, but with terrific battle scenes searing his glazing eyeballs—nor yet with the quiring of cherubim falling on his ears—but rather the tumultuous rush and deafening roar of a Liepsic or an Austerlitz. If there was in this horrid delirium of death a single momentary interval of consciousness, there must have been bitter memories of the injured Josephine who generously offered to attend him in his exile at Elba, and if she had survived would no doubt have piteously begged the privilege of nursing him in the later weary years of his imprisonment under Sir Hudson Lowe. How sharply contrasted the true wifely devotion of Josephine and the conduct of his Austrian bride, who before his death contracted a morganatic marriage below her rank as a Hapsburg princess, and yet moved as an Empress of France. In the light of Josephine's subsequent history, how strange and still how accurate the forecast of the old sybil of Martinico, who said to the jaunty Creole maiden: "You will be married soon; that union will not be happy; you will become a widow and then you will be queen of France! Some happy years will be yours, but you will die in a hospital amid civil commotion." If this statement be true, and Josephine vouched for its correctness, the aged sybil's phrophecy was almost literally fulfilled.

Before dismissing the matter of marriage and divorce in connection with the First Napoleon, it may be well to refer to his strenuous effort to induce his brothers, Lucien and Jerome, to put away their wives for selfish ends. Jerome was pliable, and for his obedience to his imperious, as well as imperial, brother, was rewarded with a petty kingdom—perhaps Westphalia. Lucien, however, was less tractable. In response to his brother's invitation, he went to the place of St. Cloud, where Napoleon was closeted with him for one or two hours, urging Lucien to give his wife and the mother of his children a bill of divorcement. Lucien was obstinate and even resentful. When his brother offered him a crown on condition that he would repudiate his wife, "a woman of gallantry," as he stigmatized her, Lucien was greatly enraged, and replied that if his wife was "a woman of gallantry," she was at least "pretty and young." This innuendo, at the expense of Josephine, fired the indignation of the Emperor, and, holding his watch in his hand, he dashed it to the floor, saying, "With like ease I could crush you as I have crushed that bauble, but you are my brother—go." Thereupon Lucien withdrew, doing honor to himself by the refusal of a crown rather than do such injustice to his wife. This whole affair shows how reckless Napoleon was of marriage obligations when they stood in the way of his ambition. It illustrates likewise another saying of the

Irish barrister, to whom we referred in the outset, that so thoroughly had Napoleon shattered the governmental institutions of Europe, "that he disposed of crowns and thrones with as little ceremomy as if they had been the titular dignitaries of a chess board.

Three Confederate officers, amongst the most conspicuous for personal gallantry in the battle of the Wilderness, were Gordon, Evans and Phil Cook, all Georgians, and all of them at this time residents of Atlanta. Speaking of General Evans, it may not be generally known that he commanded the rear guard of Lee's army during the retreat from Petersburg. In the melee his wife was captured, but luckily fell into the hands of General Custer, who treated her with great kindness and consideration, informing Evans at the first opportunity of her safety.

Custer, who was a knightly soldier, was, with his command, afterwards massacred by the Modoc Indians.

We have through the press nowadays a great deal of discussion of dietetics and pedagogics—the stomach and the school. One writer on the "curiosities of eating and drinking," justly remarks, "that every kind of food and drink is proved by some scientific discoverer or another to be rank poison." He quotes amongst others a German physiologist who claims that Buffon and Voltaire drank enormous quantities of coffee to their deadly hurt, and that "the descriptions that the former penned of the dog, the tiger and other carnivorous animals were written under strong cerebral excitement." With like confidence others aver that tea, which even Cowper drank with such gusto from the silver urn of Mr. Unwin, is a dangerous beverage to tamper with.

A dozen or more years ago, when I was oscillating between life and death, I chanced to meet an unknown gentleman who was evidently struck with my semi-cadaverous aspect. He was, I am quite sure, a learned physician from the far West. He asked me in regard to my dieting, and I informed him that I was advised to restrict myself to milk, and a small quantity of tea and vegetables. This remark seemed to startle him. "Why, my friend," he rejoined, "your medical adviser must be a very incapable personage. I insist that you should eat as much as your stomach craves of good roast beef and pork steak, washed down with liberal potations of the best whisky or brandy." "Why," said I, half smilingly, "have you forgotten that Moses prohibited swine's flesh as a sanitary measure?" "That was well enough," he answered, "when applied to the razor-back hogs around Jerusalem, but it will not hold with the Berkshires and Graziers of Kentucky and Missouri. No better diet than that for an invalid if it is properly prepared." I left the train at the next station, and taking my hand he walked to the platform of the car, and giving me a hearty hand-shaking, he said: "Don't forget the roast beef and whisky and it will make you a new man."

Only a few days ago I made an early morning call on a lady friend, and found her drinking a cup of hot water preparatory to a late breakfast. I asked if she found any virtue in it. She replied that it was the best medicine she had ever tried for indigestion. She drank it so hot that it almost blistered her tongue. And yet chemists inform us that pepsin, the most important ingredient of the gastric juice, is rendered inert and valueless for digestive purposes when fluids are taken into the stomach of a higher temperature than 120 or 130° Fahrenheit. Such is the great uncertainty touching this whole question of diet and medication.

Our own conviction is that instinct, or whatever else it may be called, is the safest guide in this matter of eating and drinking. If a man has, like Sir Roger de Coverly, "a roast beef stomach," let him tackle a sirloin; if his stomach craves cheese, let him call for it, even if it be sweitzer. If he relishes a plate of turtle soup or a cup of black coffee, let him have it according to his liking. The brutes find their medicine in herbs and grasses, and possibly never make a mistake, and likewise as to their food unless it is tampered with. In cases of willful or accidental poisoning, their instinct stands them as little in stead as man's higher reason avails him under like circumstances.

We reserve to another time what we may wish to say on the subject of pedagogics, which we referred to in the outset of this "penciling."

Some unknown friend has placed us under obligations by sending me a pamphlet copy of the alumni address of Col. N. J. Hammond. It is issued by *The Constitu-*

tion job office, and in the best style of the typographic art. Elsewhere we have spoken in a general way of the merits of the address. We propose now to illustrate the correctness of our former statement by reproducing a single brief but striking passage which will serve as a fair sample of the whole address :

It is a grand thing to have the courage of one's convictions. Three examples stand out in sacred history to teach this noble courage. Joshua proclaiming that whatever Israel may decide " as for me and my house we will serve the Lord;" Daniel worshipping after the proclamation of the king to the contrary, just as he did before; and Paul saying he would go to Jerusalem in spite of the warning of Agabus and the fears and entreaties of his friends. No less in business affairs and politics than in religion is such a quality admirable. He inspires confidence who hesitates not when duty calls, to stake the presidency upon a message.

But some will say that such conduct will bring defeat. That depends upon what we mean by defeat. If mere ephemeral success be all that is hoped for, if the best role is that of the trimmer, and the missing of the temporary rewards of such conduct be want of success, they are right. But

"Not in the clamor of the crowded street,
But in ourselves are triumph and defeat."

When Burke was taunted that the Whig party had been disgracefully beaten, he replied : " O illustrious disgrace! O victorious defeat! May your memorial be fresh and new to the latest generation. * * * Let no man hear of us who shall not hear that in a struggle against the intrigues of courts, and the perfidious levity of the multitude, we fell in the cause of honor, in the cause of our country, in the cause of humanity itself. But if fortune should be as powerful over fame as she has been over virtue, at least our conscience is beyond her jurisdiction."

"Honest" Hugh Latimer, of immortal memory, was wiser than some preachers of the present generation, in that he believed in a "personal devil." Not a few have outgrown this article of the creed and are disposed, like Burns, to poke fun, and now and then to extend sympathy to "old Splayfoot," as Sam Jones has christened him. Barring the occasional profanity, Burns' "Address to the Deil," is one of the best serio comic poems of British literature. How widely different the conception of that "rhyming, ranting bardie" from the portrait of Milton in "Paradise Lost." That council of pandemonium in which Mammon, Moloch and Belial, and Satan himself, debate in parliamentary style the burning issues of war and peace, reads like a page of modern history in which the Castlereaghs, Metternichs and Talleyrands figure in high diplomatic discussion.

Some critics are not far wrong who say that the devil is the hero of the great English epic. Compared with him, the lesser devils are dwarfed into pigmies. In like manner Adam is reduced to the level of a country squire, and Eve, the mother of us all, is a commonplace personage, except when departing from Eden she breaks forth into that superb apostrophe to the lost Paradise with its nuptial bowers and its beautifully graded walks, which remind us of some of the best work of the landscape gardener. Addison was the first English writer to popularize "Paradise Lost," which else had fallen still born from the press. In these latter days it is frequently talked of, but seldom read. I fairly devoured it fifty years ago, but I question if in the last twenty years I have read a hundred consecutive lines at a sitting. My experience in this line is not exceptional. The shorter poems of Milton, such as "L'Allegro and Il Penseroso," "Comus" and the sonnets are still read, and the same remark applies to some of his prose writings.

But, it may be asked, what has all this to do with the devil? We might reply in the words of St. Paul, with reference to another matter, "Much every way, chiefly because the Satan of the orthodox creed is perhaps quite as much Miltonic as scriptural. We do not mean to concede that the scriptures do not teach clearly and impressively the fact that there is a being, if you please, "an arch-angel ruined," who is the great adversary of Christ and his kingdom. Nor, as St. Peter says, are the enlightened "ignorant of his wiles." How far he may be suffered to impress and influence human destiny is not fully revealed. But of this we are assured, that "if we resist him he will flee from us."

The oldest man probably since Mathuselah was a Tyrolese peasant, who was born in the seventeenth century and survived the storming of the bastile and the downfall of the French monarchy. A visit which he made to Paris is described by Carlyle in his history of the French revolution. He was granted almost as striking an ovation as was Voltaire on his last visit to Paris. How checkered the experiences of a centenarian! If compiled, what a volume they would make! What a blending of smiles and tears! What a jumble of tragic and comic scenes! What a mixture of pathos and pleasantry! But greater still the manifold experiences of a man who lived nine hundred and sixty and nine years. Is the scriptural chronology at fault? If we remember that the Hebrew writers had neither Arabic nor Roman numerals, we see how mistakes might have occurred.

We may form some idea of the immense longevity of Mathuselah, if we compare his age with that of the British Empire. The old Hebrew patriarch might have fought at Hastings in 1066, and lived on until the last Plantagenet was entombed at Westminster. He would have been in the prime of life during the Wars of the Roses, and might have witnessed the funeral obsequies of Elizabeth, the last of the Tudor line. He would have been but little past middle life when Marlborough fought and won at Blenheim, and when Anne of Denmark, the last of the Stuarts, gave way to the house of Hanover, and thus on and on until now he would be somewhat gray and wrinkled, and yet in a fair way to see the close of the twentieth century. The brain reels under the weight of such a computation, and we are disposed to thank the gracious One that now fixes four score years as the limit of man's life-pilgrimage.

Ex-Senator Strother, of Lincoln, is known to be a great admirer of the ladies, but it is not so generally known that he has a passion for mathematics, especially the calculus integral and differential. After talking with him quite awhile on that subject I switched him off on Longstreet's story of the dark corner of Lincoln in the "Georgia Scenes." He says that this famous locality is in the Southeastern corner of the county where it abuts on the Savannah river, and only about thirty miles distant from Augusta. The hero of the tale was one Shade Wethers, a sort of happy-go-lucky wight, who was excessively fond of strong drink. He was anything but a bully himself, being a very inoffensive personage. But Wethers, like Ransy Sniffle, had a keen relish for a cross roads fisticuff, and would often walk to the court house on muster or election days that he might witness any exhibition of the kind which should turn up. He was in this mood probably when he improvised the private theatricals in the skirt of woods through which Longstreet passed on his way to Lincolnton. From the amount of cussing and cavorting made by Wethers, Longstreet thought that he was in a stone's cast of a Donnybrook fair, and when the Judge turned aside to read the riot act or command the peace, he was amazed to find but a single actor in the melee.

Wethers, as the Judge states, put on a hang-dog look when he demanded of him where his antagonist was.

He naively replied that he was "jest'er seeing how he could have fout." It was for printing such humorous and sketches as this that some of the strait-breasted Methodist clergy, like Uncle John Collinsworth, who voted against licensing George Pierce to preach, were inclined to call Judge Longstreet to account at the bar of the conference. Senator Strother protests that the militia muster, of which Oliver H Prince contributed an account to the Georgia Scenes, did not occur in Lincoln, but in Wilkes. He is probably jealous of the honor of the county which he has so ably represented.

Our Pat Calhoun is clearly "a chip of the old block." We do not accept his subtreasury views, but, take his address to the Legislature in its totality, and it is characterized by a vigor of thought and terseness of statement that reminds us of that great Carolinian who met and triumphantly refuted the great Webster in their joint discussion of the States' rights resolutions in 1834. We are certainly influenced by no personal considerations in this estimate, for our acquaintance with Mr. Pat Calhoun does not go beyond a single introduction.

Queen Victoria conferred a baronetcy on General Havelock for his gallant services during the Sepoy rebellion. But the merited honor came too late, for that noble Christian warrior had died three weeks before the distinction was bestowed. The next best thing was done in conferring the title on his oldest son, a young man of rare promise and of splendid character.

At one period of his life John C. Calhoun dominated the thought and politics of South Carolina as fully as did Pericles the thought of Athens in its palmiest days. So that it become a proverb, coarse but expressive, that when Mr. Calhoun took snuff the whole State from Pickens' Nose to Charleston would sneeze. Hammond and Pettigru and a few others were possible exceptions, but the one man who was his peer in scholarship and intellectual compass, and who boldly antagonized his theory of government, was Hugh Swinton Legare, the head and front of Whigism in that Jeffersonian stronghold. As David B. Hill proclaims "I am a Democrat," so Legare thanked God "that he was a Huguenot." His educational opportunities were of the best. In early boyhood he was a pupil of Waddell at the Willington Academy in Abbeville district. From thence he went to the State College at Columbia, where he graduated with the highest distinction. From Columbia he went to Edinburgh, having Preston for his fellow collegian. In that far-famed university he took high rank, and was occasionally brought in personal contact with the great lights of "Auld Reekie," the center of learning in Great Britain. After a good deal of continental travel he returned to Charleston and opened a law office, and at the age of forty-five was Attorney-General of the United States. He died three years thereafter in Boston, at the house of his bosom friend, Ticknor, whose studies in Spanish literature have been an honor to his country.

We have reproduced these biographic details partly

to illustrate the facility with which a very great man may be forgotten, but chiefly as preparatory to a more important statement, that but for the opposition of Legare and Pettigru to the nullification movement South Carolina might have precipitated a dissolution of the Union thirty years before the first gun was fired at Sumter. In that event we might long ere this have had two sister republics side by side in good working order. On such slight contingencies very often hinge the fate of great men and the destiny of vast empires.

Poor Goldsmith had at times a misanthropic mood, or perhaps we ought to say a fit of nervous depression that beclouded his usually sunny temper. It was at such a time doubtless that he penned that hackneyed quartrain—

> "What is friendship but a name?
> A charm that lulls to sleep,
> A shade that follows wealth or fame
> And leaves the wretch to weep."

There are many faithless ones in all circles, but the above sentiment is too broad a generalization. That man has been indeed singularly unfortunate whose experience does not contradict this pessimistic statement. It is not every day that we encounter a "fidus Achates," nor are we apt to stumble with even less frequency on a friendship like that which knit the souls of David and Jonathan. And yet we ourselves must be quite undeserving if we have not on our list of friends, a goodly number, who have never faltered in their devotion to us and our fortunes. These life-long friendships do not always have their root in similarity of tastes. As opposite electricities attract each other, so differences of mental and physical temperament will often bind men together as with "hooks of steel."

Goldsmith and Johnson were unlike in very many respects, and yet there is no reason to question that Goldsmith loved his illustrious friend, however he was worried by his dogmatism—nor is there any reason to doubt that this affection was reciprocated.

Some of the ablest writers for the religious press are beginning to realize that the multiplication of societies for various moral purposes is likely to prove a hindrance to the church in its legitimate work. The danger seems imminent that the church will be cumbered and weighed down by a superabundance of machinery. Nor is it less to be feared that individual Christian efforts will be weakened or utterly paralyzed. The "fad" comes from New England, where, amongst some good things, many evil things are wont to originate. The colored brother has caught the infection, and we see processions with badges and banners moving through our streets, bearing such unique inscriptions as these: "The Weeping Sons of Jacob," and "The Mourning Doves of Zion." To take a single illustration of our main thought, almsgiving, which is an eminent virtue and an obvious personal duty, is relegated to benevolent associations, to the serious detriment of the pious giver. The Apostle James has given us the best Scriptural definition of religion. "True religion and undefiled * * * is to visit the fatherless and the widow in their affliction, and to keep himself unspotted from the world." The word visit in the text is not put there by accident, but for a wise purpose. It involves the idea of personal contact with human want and wretchedness. It enjoins something beyond the mere bestowment of money, needful as that may be. It implies a personal visitation, during which there shall be the expression of sympathy for the sufferer and an earnest endeavor by word and look to uplift the forlorn and shipwrecked brother.

It was wise in the Apostle Peter, when he would relieve the impotent man at the beautiful gate of the temple, to take him by the hand and lift him up. The Apostolic touch thrilled the poor fellow and put him in a receptive mood, so that he was ready to respond to the foregone commandment, "In the name of Jesus Christ of Nazareth rise up and walk" Is it strange that immediately he rose and stood erect, and walked and even leaped? It was in allusion to this incident that Erasmus said to Leo X. that the church of the sixteenth century had lost its power to make the lame man rise up and walk. The church of to-day is only in a less measure shorn of its strength from like causes. It affects cushioned pews, frescoed walls and carpeted aisles; it withdraws itself from the company of publicans and sinners. Outside of the Salvation Army and the half-starved missionary, it leaves the poor and the friendless to drift away from Heaven and happiness.

It doles out a pittance by proxy, but never soils itself

by closer contact with the dependent classes. If I were called upon to say who, of the priesthood, had in these latter days exhibited the most Christ-like spirit, I should without hesitancy name Father Damien, who ministered to the leprous community of the Sandwich Islands. His theology was little better than that of St. Dominic, the founder of the Inquisition, but his religion was like that of Jesus of Nazareth, the Son of God and the Saviour of men.

I remember in my boyhood attending a Harrison meeting, where Dr. DeGraffenried, of Columbus, Ga., the father of our Marshall DeGraffenried, was one of the speakers. The "Tip and Ty" excitement was just developing into the political freshet that revolutionized the country. The doctor was a Virginia gentleman of the old school, and, like Judge W. H. Underwood, an avowed federalist. He had just returned from a northern tour, and was describing the uprising of the masses for the old farmer of North Bend. The report electrified his Whig audience, and the applause was deafening. Amongst other palpable hits was his saying that from Augusta, where he crossed the State line, to Columbus, he had passed through but one county that would poll a majority for Van Buren, and that was Trout county. Some party friend interrupted the speaker with the suggestion that it was Pike, not Trout county. The old doctor paused for a moment, and added in a sort of parenthesis: "Well," said he, "I knew it was some blank fish county!" The uproar of laughter that followed can be better imagined than described. Nothing like that log cabin campaign has been seen since in Georgia. The present alliance movement is a tame affair in comparison.

It was during the premiership of Disraeli that a mitred dignitary of the English church was remarking on the perverseness of a brilliant young clergyman. Said his grace, with evident concern: "He is manifestly verging on Puseyism, and I am at a loss as to the proper disposition to be made of him." The great tory leader responded: "If you will make him a Bishop, you will cure his doctrinal vagaries." The proposed remedy was tested, and proved effectual. Official promotion, whether in church or state, is quite sure to correct erratic tendencies.

The old Romans had a saying that if a citizen had children he had given hostages to the republic. With rare exceptions, the ranks of communism are recruited from those classes that are badly conditioned. A small freehold is apt to make a man conservative in his political views. Village attorneys were, indeed, prominent in the French revolution, but the men that stormed the Bastile, and did the bidding of Robespiere, were the *sans-cullotic* rabble of the slums. Well-to-do people are not likely, except under great provocation, to rush into riot and revolution.

"Duruy's History of Rome" is the most exhaustive work of its kind that has fallen under our notice.

This French author has completed the work which Niebuhr began, but left unfinished. No portion of the six volumes of this elaborate history is of greater importance than that which relates to the period of the two great triumvirates. Especially do his admirable portraitures of Cicero, Cataline, Pompey and Julius Cæsar almost compensate for the lost books of Livy. His explanation of the causes of the decay of agriculture in the Italian peninsula is a sort of historical revelation. He argues that with a tariff system like the English corn laws, the empire would not have fallen so easy a prey to the northern barbarians. It was certainly an alarming condition of affairs when the world's great capital was dependent for its food supplies on corn ships from Egypt, Sardinia, Sicily and remoter countries. It was a fearful aggravation when one of the twelve Cæsars ordered some of the ships at Alexandria to be loaded with sand for the arena, making the then existing scarcity more stringent and appalling. This was but the prelude to the dark days of the latter empire. Can it be that the corrupt political methods of these evil days are preparing our own country for a like doom and destiny?

There is a small class of educationists whose crankiness borders on lunacy. These have told us that in the late Franco-Prussian war Germany conquered France by the Pestalozzian system of education. They make but little account of the military drill and discipline bequeathed by the great Frederick, or of the admirable transportation service organized by Moltke and Bismarck.

How does this view comport with the admitted fact that, perhaps, the best fighting troops of modern Europe were the illiterate boy conscripts, that Napoleon gathered out of the lanes and alleys of Paris and Marseilles? Verily, those learned Thebans are hobby-horsical in their habits.

One Lossing, who writes history for the youth, in a contribution to the *New York Independent*, lectures Dr. Curry and Bishop Haygood for characterizing the little unpleasantness that ended at Appomattox as a "war between the States." He thinks the right term is rebellion—written in capitals. We wish that our people would boycott all such writers.

Asbury Hull, Elbridge G Cabiness and R. A. T. Ridley were typical Whigs of the anti-bellum days. They were close, personal friends and trusted counselors of Berrien, Crawford, Toombs and Stephens. All of them were prominent figures in Georgia politics. One thing was strikingly characteristic of these followers of Henry Clay They were noted for their personal cleanliness. Zeb Vance, who had a knack of saying sharp things, used to say that the Whigs as a class wore standing collars, well polished boots and claw-hammer coats. In a word they had the appearance of gentlemen, and even a bit of the true nobleman look. Asbury

Hull, who died a few years ago in Athens, while reading his morning lesson in the scriptures, was chosen two or more times as President of the Senate. Cabiness was a circuit judge and chairman of the State Executive Committee during the Gordon and Bullock campaign. Ridley several times represented the grand old county of Troup in the State Legislature, was more than once on the Whig electoral ticket and was a bosom friend of Ben Hill. They were all staunch church members. Hull and Ridley Methodists and Cabiness a Baptist. Let it not be inferred, however, that the Clay and Everett Whigs had a monopoly of the decencies or elegancies of this remote period. On the contrary, there were such men as Walter H. Mitchell, Henry Todd and Dr. Joel Branham, who were Democrats of the straitest sect. Walter H. Mitchell was the father of the first wife of Chief Justice Jackson, and was for years a prominent State House official at the old capitol. Henry Todd was a wealthy planter, residing near West Point, who eschewed office-seeking. Joel Branham was a Middle Georgia physician of great distinction. They were all educated, and of the best lineage. In one respect they were all men of note amongst their contemporaries. As conversationalists and story tellers of the old school, they had few superiors. Indeed you must needs go a long journey to find two men who could better entertain a dinner party than Todd and Mitchell, when in their best mood. Branham was at times quite as felicitous in the same role; and then, as a political stump speaker, he had few equals in his generation. By a singular coincidence they were all Methodists, and great admirers of Lovick Pierce, Sam Anthony and Billy Parks. Men of the class we have mentioned have no successors. The changes in political and social conditions have prevented this, but their descendants are amongst our most worthy and honored citizens.

When Lord Cardigan was ordered to charge the Russian batteries at Balaklava, he instantly sprung to his saddle, and putting himself at the head of the column, he shouted in a ringing voice: "Forward, the Light Brigade." As the column, with dancing plumes and glittering sabers, dashed forward at a hand gallop, the brave commander said to his nearest staff officer: "Here goes the last of the Cardigans." And yet such are the fortunes of war that he was one of the few of rank that came out of the "jaws of hell," unscathed by sword or bullet.

It has been said that the order that brought about this terrible sacrifice of human life was a forgery—Lord Lucan denying that he ever signed such an order. This example, however, of heoric daring was worth all that it cost. It will hold its place in history with the conduct of the three hundred that kept the pass at Thermopylæ and of McDonald's division with its magnificent charge at Wagram. These transcendental feats of bravery make the brightest pages in the annals of war. They lift it above the low level of brute courage and savage ferocity and invest it with the iridescent hues of the noblest exhibitions of chivalry as chronicled by Froissart or as chanted in epic strains by "the blind old Bard of Scio's rocky isle." After all, war is not of necessity an unmitigated social evil. As the tempest purifies the atmosphere, clearing it of deadly malaria, so the shock of battle brings out some of the best qualities of genuine manhood which otherwise would have lain dormant and unknown. An occasional blood-letting purges alike the body natural and the body politic of vicious humors. Quakerism has never developed the highest style of Christian civilization.

Some one has designated Victor Hugo in thoroughly French phraseology as the "enfant sublime," and yet it is on record by the family physician, or perhaps his mother, that at his birth he was not longer than a breakfast knife, with a life expectation hardly worth the labor of computation. But he survived the perils of infancy, became a peer of France and a writer unequaled by any European contemporary. Political troubles drove him from his native land in 1851 and shut him up in the island of Guernsey, one of the five channel islands best known for their superb breed of milch cows. In this literary seclusion he wrote his masterpieces, "Les Miserables" and "The Toilers of the Sea." It was in the former that he discussed John Brown's murderous raid on Harper's Ferry. It was a singular misapprehension which led him to discover an analogy between this foray of Brown and the battle of Bunker Hill. The object of Brown and his aiders and abettors was plunder and rapine. It is not credible that he hoped in any degree to better the condition of the slaves. The most charitable construction of the affair is that he was a monomaniac, who was used by the abolition leaders to precipitate a sectional struggle that might bring them official position and personal emolument. It is not to be wondered at that Gerrit Smith, who had instigated the movement, lost his head when informed of Brown's disastrous failure and his subsequent execution. It is difficult to believe that Brown's entire force consisted of but seventeen whites and three negroes. He, however, counted largely on recruits from the Virginia slaves, but these recruits did not materialize.

There is no room for questioning John Brown's courage. That was shown on the hottest battlefields of Kansas when, as at Lawrence, Ossawatomie and Black Jack, he distinguished himself as an intrepid and skillful partisan leader. He met his doom under the gallows tree with stolid indifference. The story of his kissing the child of the slave-mother at the foot of the scaffold is sheer fiction, but it is true according to the testimony of eye-witnesses that as he ascended the steps of the gallows he showed the courage of his convictions. When asked by the sheriff to take a handkerchief and drop it as a signal when he was ready, he replied that he "did not want it, but do not," he added, "keep me longer than is necessary."

Since his death it has been claimed that his ancestors came over in the Mayflower. Whether this be an after-thought invented by those who would invest his brow with the aureole of the martyr it is quite evident that he had a measure of the pluck and persistence of the old Puritan warriors that fought under Cromwell and Ireton. This Harper's Ferry raid was the initial chapter of the war between the states and only antedated the first gun at Sumter by about eighteen months.

Before finally dismissing the subject, we recur to our statement that the slave population in the vicinity of Harper's Ferry kept aloof from any complicity with the movement. The colored troops are accredited by Northern histories with "fighting nobly" on some occasions, but this usually occurred when there were bayonets at their backs to urge them forward. At Harper's Ferry, the Virginia darkey had no fancy for handling John Brown's pikes. We find in an old Baltimore magazine this reminiscence of one who was on the ground: "One sturdy fellow said that when he was taken a pike was put into his hand, and the old abolitionist exhorted him to 'strike for liberty.'" "Good Lord, Massa," cried Cuffy in a tremor, "I don't know nuffin' about handlin' these tings." "Take it instantly," shouted Brown, "and strike home." The negro couldn't see the point, however. "Don't you know me?" cried Brown. "Didn't you never hear of John Brown, of Ossawatomie?" This frightened the negroes all the more, and they fled to the hayricks and other places of refuge for shelter. This writer expresses the belief that they would then and there have fought at the bidding of their old master.

Our friend, Mr. J. H. Rucker, furnishes another California story of a graver tone than that concerning Bill Jones and his Jersey sweetheart. At Gold Hill, which was Mr. Rucker's mining headquarters, religious services were seldom conducted by the ministry. At longer or shorter intervals a preacher would come that way, and all classes would importune him to give them an appointment. On one occasion a Methodist minister consented to preach, and as there was neither chapel nor suitable hall in the village, the landlord of the hotel improvised a desk in front of the bar, where wines and stronger beverages were sold by the single drink or the quart.

A congregation of fifty or more assembled at the hour appointed for the service. The minister having sung and prayed, was proceeding to announce his text, when two well known and much dreaded desperadoes, partially intoxicated, appeared upon the scene. They seemed bent on some deviltry, as with a swaggering and defiant air they demanded drinks of the bartender. Everybody knew that a refusal of their demand might lead to riot and bloodshed. The minister paused without exhibiting any signs of trepidation. The bartender quietly directed them to help themselves, which they did in presence of the preacher and congregation. Having each imbibed a half pint or more, they deliberately walked away. Out of ear-shot, the minister went on with his sermon without further molestation. Such scenes, many of them more turbulent, not unfrequently occurred in the mining regions in those early days of

California history. The preachers of that day did not wear a sword, but they were, emphatically, militant saints, and on rare occasions were forced to resort to carnal weapons for self protection. The late Dr. Jesse Boring was engaged in this pioneer work for several years, and many of his California adventures and experiences ought to be perpetuated in book form. Bishop Fitzgerald and Rev. R. W. Bigham have both contributed some very readable volumes to the literature of this subject.

General John H. Morgan was no "literary feller" as Simon Cameron phrases it, but a lively fighter, who stirred up things generally beyond the Ohio. At one time he visited Atlanta, being chaperoned by Colonel Bob Alston, himself a dashing cavalier. Morgan was a man of majestic stature, and of a personal daring and a personal magnetism that fitted him to head a forlorn hope in the crisis of battle. He was greeted in Atlanta with great enthusiasm, and especially by the female citizenry. During his stay quite a number of our most prominent ladies wished to present him with a beautiful gold-headed cane, upon which he might lean, after he had hung up his battered sword in the halls of victory. A gentleman well-known to the writer was asked to make a short presentation speech. Consenting to do so, he thought it proper to see the General and inform him of the programme. When the General learned that a reply would be expected from him, he turned pale and red by turns and said to the gentleman : " My dear sir, I am no speaker and I had rather storm a yankee battery than to make a speech." At his earnest request the programme was changed—so that the cane was handed him with a note in behalf of the ladies. To this he made a very tasteful written reply. The ladies, however, called on him in a body. He conversed very pleasantly with them for some fifteen minutes. During this interview a young miss was toying with the handkerchief in the General's coat pocket, and by some legerdemain succeeded in extracting it. The General was evidently conscious of the mischief, but good-humoredly feigned ignorance. After the ladies retired the handkerchief was torn into strips and distributed amongst the party. My lady informant tells me that she kept hers as a sort of souvenir of the General's visit for some years, until it was misplaced and lost.

A much admired conversationalist of the olden times once said that "conversation between more than two persons was an impossibility." This disposes of table talk and other babblement of a convivial kind Addison's statement was perhaps too strong, but it is unquestionably true that a conversation *tete-a-tete* is preferable to the din of the city club, or the buzz of the village sewing circle. In these promiscuous gatherings cheekiness rather than brains takes the leadership, and the Gratiano "who talks an infinite deal of nothing," carries the crowd. To soliloquize is one thing and to converse, as the terms imply, is quite another thing. Coleridge was a great success in the former *role;* so was

Madam de Stael, the daughter of Necker, who would, at times, monopolize both the big and small talk of a Parisian *salon*. Most persons have, at times, encountered the monologist, who would put the "Ancient Mariner" to the blush. Think of a man with an important engagement staring him in the face, who is abruptly button-holed at the street corner and constrained to listen to a dry narrative of a half-hour's length. Some years ago we had a carload of Northern visitors at one of the State fairs. Albert Lamar, who was not in the best humor with these visiting brethren, remarked that he was glad they were to be entertained by Colonel ——, who was distinguished for his exuberant loquacity. Lamar said that it was a sweet revenge for the downfall of the Confederacy. "Live and let live" is a good motto in conversation as in business. Give your patient listener credit for knowing something.

Is there either "rhyme or reason" in this clangor of church bells on Sabbath morning? When watches are so cheap and steeple clocks are so numerous, cannot the congregation assemble without the summons of a notice bell? We are aware that Cowper wrote something touching about the sound of "the church-going bell," and other bards of a melancholy bent have sentimentalized about the bells of Shandon and of St. Petersburg. Indeed somebody has ventured the incredible statement that Napoleon halted in mid-career on a hilltop to listen to the bells of Brienne. This may be poetical, but it is puerile. Why rack the nerves of sick people on a week night or break the stillness of the holy day by the "wrangling and the jangling of the bells, bells, bells?" Poe and Schiller seemed to have had a reverence for bells, but both were slightly daft.

As a means of assembling the faithful on the patriotic we prefer the Muezzin's call or the stentorian shout of the old-fashioned town-crier.

IN A SICK CHAMBER.—There is a singular fascination for most readers in that sort of literature which savors of autobiography. Hence the vast popularity of such works as "Cæsar's Commentaries," "The Confession of St. Augustine," and "Bishop Burnett's History of His Own Time." The same holds good in regard to fictive literature, such as the "Jane Eyre," of Miss Bronte, and the "David Copperfield," of Dickens, where the sitter and the artist are the same person. I find myself, as I grow older, likely to fall into this autobiographic strain, as will appear in this paper, dictated in a sick chamber. On the 4th of March instant, my sixty-fifth birthday, I was closely shut in by stress of weather and a thoroughly orthodox attack of la grippe. Not a slight nasal catarrh, but such an attack as might suggest to the sufferer the hug of a grizzly, or the grasp of a devil fish; an attack involving both the anterior and posterior nares, both eyes and ears; the *meatus auditorius externus* throbbing and buzzing as if the Anvil Chorus was being played in the next room. Shade of Esculapius! Was such an influenza known in the infancy of medical science? It will be observed that my own birthday and that of Robert Emmet, the young Irish patriot, fall upon the same day of the calendar, the inauguration day of the American Presidents. Thinking of Emmet, I recall a dramatic representation of the trial scene of the young patriot at Hamilton, Ga. As I distinctly remember, Colonel W. C. Osborn, the village Boniface, personated Lord Norbury, the presiding justice. A bright young lawyer of the village, a nephew of old Governor Strong, of Massachusetts, enacted the part of young Emmet with brilliant success. After the applause which followed the delivery of Emmet's notable defense, another cultured gentleman rose and recited, most touchingly, the lines of the Irish bard inscribed to the memory of Miss Curran, the *fiancee* of the Irish martyr, beginning:

"She is far from the land where her young hero sleeps."

These lines are, perhaps, the best, certainly the tenderest of Moore's melodies, saving that other beginning:

"Come rest in this bosom, my own stricken dear."

It is a lamentable fact that Emmet's epitaph is still unwritten, in the closing decade of the nineteenth century. Nor is it likely to be written for another half century, if that greatest living Englishman, Gladstone, is to be handicapped by such a marplot as Charles Stewart Parnell. My charming amanuensis, who had written thus far, remarked that she preferred Moore's sacred songs to any of his other melodies. Not bad taste, we replied, for he wrote nothing better than

"Come, Ye Disconsolate." Strange besides, that a devotee of fashion and frivolity should have written a poem whose pious sentiment should have so deeply touched the religious sensibilities of mankind.

There are lights as well as shadows in a sick chamber. To say nothing of rare delicacies, kindly sent by gentle friends, that might coax an appetite when sorely impaired by disease, and then fruits ard flowers that bring the sunlight and autumn into the closely curtained chamber. But there are better things than even the presence and prayers of godly visitors, clerical and lay. Likewise, occasional letters from distant friends full of brotherly sympathy. Witness the following that reached me amidst a steady downpour from a leaden sky. I was feeling like Romeo when the friar told him he was "wedded to calamity," when this sunburst broke on me.

C——, March 9, 1891.—Dear Brother Scott: My habit is to read everything from your pen, and of you; so I thought much and prayed about you when I read a notice of your illness in some paper a week ago. I hope you are "over it" now—"about again." Your pen has been of exceeding usefulness in taking readers into religious growth and light where men are not apt to look for them, and in a way so charming and unusual as to make them absorb the religious and the literary, put in the scholarly style. May only good come to you, and constantly.

Somehow the things that seem fittest don't come to pass. I have thought that the *Nashville Christian Advocate*, in your care the last eight years, would have set things forward in the connection. You are Wesleyan, with the addition of the light of the century since Wesley died. You think, and have thought clear, greater than the average great things the papers have needed for the people. You are broad without mockery for the narrow, and religious without posing for its fame. I have often thought, too, that many years ago I was wiser in urging you to transfer to New Orleans, and do for Methodism there what Dr. Palmer did for Presbyterianism, than you were in declining. By now you would have had us to the front there. Yet, who knows? Yours may have been quite the wiser after all. And "the lines" you have wrought in your lifework may be those whose light shall shine farthest and best.

May God keep you to the end. It is after "the end" that one's record is entered up and the true "well done" pronounced. If I could bless you, old comrade, I would pray our God comfort, heal, renew your life, bless you for me.   Yours truly,

———.

We withhold the name, with the single statement that it was a love-token from a minister and author of much distinction. It is a model of letter-writing.

Dr. H. V. M. Miller, who is perhaps the brainiest man in half a dozen states, spent an hour with me a few days ago. I was struck with one observation. Said he, "Scott, you know that it is the extremist that carries the day in a political contest." This single remark opened the way to much talk about Cromwell and his saints, who ejected the Presbyterians from the long parliament. This quite naturally suggested the stubborn fight between the Girondists and Jacobins—ending in the utter overthrow of the former. Next in order, the contest between the conservatives and the secessionists, winding up with the dismemberment of the Union and a war between the states. Then the conflict between President Johnson and the congressional majority, as to the mode of reconstruction. Andrew Johnson was near losing his official head, and Thad Stevens and his gang were left masters of the situation. "What bearing has this," said Miller, "on the pending struggle between Livingston and Northen?" I only replied in the language of Father Ritchie, "*Nous verrons.*"

"Liberty Hall" was properly named, for Mr. Stephens kept open house for all comers. On two occasions I was a guest of the great commoner, and was accorded the freedom of the old-style mansion. His hospitality was not lavish, as measured by dinner courses or servants in livery, but there was a gracious welcome and a *menu* that was toothsome and abundant.

During my two visits I had an opportunity of studying the character of this great man when he was free from conventional restraints, and in some sort *en deshabille*. I could but notice that because of his delicate organism he was exceedingly impressible by atmospheric changes. He watched the mercury in his thermometer with very great interest. He would frequently shift his chair from one room to another, and from the veranda to the hall. Let it not be inferred, however, that he was in the least annoyed by hypochondriac fancies. On the contrary, notwithstanding his physical weakness and his frequent bodily sufferings, he was uniformly cheerful and at times buoyant in spirits. His conversation, in his lighter moods, was seasoned with genuine attic salt, and enlivened with incidents oftentimes exquisitely humorous.

On one occasion, I asked him to give me his impressions of some of the foremost of his congressional associates of ante-bellum days. I can recall but a few of these graphic word portraits. He regarded Thad Stevens as a man of massive brain with a lack of literary culture, and a dash of coarseness in his composition. He thought his political integrity was unimpeachable, but his anti-slavery sentiments sometimes amounted to a political craze. Billy Allen, of Ohio, had a similar moral and mental make-up, except that Allen was a Democrat of the Jacksonian type. Tom Corwin, of the same state, he thought, had few equals in a rough-and-tumble debate, whether on the floor of Congress or on the hustings. Henry Clay, as might be supposed, was his ideal of a statesman. Webster, he esteemed as the greater constitutional lawyer, but inferior to Calhoun in philosophical range of intellect. Seward, of New York, he considered one of the cleverest thinkers and readiest debaters of the United States Senate. His friend

Toombs, however, he regarded as easily first as a senatorial speaker when he had a great theme and a momentous occasion.

I remember nothing in my personal experience equal in interest to these off-hand sketches in this simple conversation of the sage of Liberty Hall. Amongst other anecdotes which he related, there was one that will bear repetition. He was engaged in a very important trial in Greene Superior Court. After the case had been argued and the jury had retired, he accepted the invitation of a wealthy Whig planter to spend the night with him at his country residence, some five miles from the village. Just at sunset the planter drove up to Mr. Stephens's hotel with a spanking team of blooded horses. Mr. Stephens took his seat, and his friend, with a word to his horses and a tap on the withers of the leader, started at a 2:40 pace. They had gone but a short distance when Mr. Stephens became a little nervous, and demurred at such a rate of speed. His friend said to him, "Aleck, I always suffer you to do my thinking in politics, but when it comes to driving horses I propose to do my own thinking." Mr. Stephens says he saw that remonstrance was fruitless and accordingly accepted the situation. Of course everything went well, and in due time he was safely seated at the hospitable board of the planter. My last interview with Mr. Stephens was at the residence of Dr. Setze, of Marietta, Ga. He was then on his crutches, but had lost none of his mental vivacity nor his relish for an occasional potation of "pure Jeffersonian Democracy," nor his liking for a game of whist, which almost invariably followed his evening cup of tea.

Hundreds of people have heard of Edmund Burke's great speech on the trial of Warren Hastings. It was only eclipsed by Sheridan's thrilling effort, which produced such a sensation in the house that a motion to adjourn was unanimously carried, because that body was in no mood to transact business. A lesser number have likewise read Burke's brilliant essay on the "Sublime and Beautiful," one of the masterpieces of English belles letters. Not a few have read of his sparkling bon mots, at the Turk's Head, where he was esteemed the best talker in a club that numbered Johnson and Garrick and Goldsmith and lesser lights among its members.

But how many know of a fact that Thackeray has recorded that going home from the club one night Burke was accosted by a fallen woman, and was so moved by her tears, that he carried her to the house of his own wife and children, and kept her there until he could place her where she was restored to virtue and industry. This was a greater honor to the illustrious statesman than his greatest forensic efforts or his noble letter to his Bristol constituents. And then how Christly the conduct of that London grocer, of whom Spurgeon tells us. This good Samaritan devoted his money largely to the rescuing of this unfortunate class. At the door of his business place he posted this invitation: "If there be any unfortunate sister who is without a home, and desires to do better, let her apply within." It was estimated that 150 of the Magdalens of the great metropolis were reclaimed from a life of shame and wretchedness by his efforts. Individual charity of this kind is good to lead the way in this and similar enterprises, but it is simply preparatory to organized effort, which, rightly conducted, will accomplish grand results.

Atlanta needs a "home" for this class, and the time is ripe for its establishment. Let it be inaugurated under proper auspices and its success is assured. In this way, and in no other, we may extract the sting of Tom Hood's reproach, which applies to every city of 50,000 inhabitants, that has made no such provision:

> "O, it was pitiful,
> Near a whole city full,
> Home she had none."

The shooting of Chief, the crazy elephant, was a monstrous cruelty. Where, we might ask, were the Humane Societies that funeralize a dead ass, and sit up of nights with a sick monkey, when this murder was perpetrated, without an indignant protest? If there be a Heaven, as John Wesley more than hinted, for birds and beasts, then surely this emperor of quadrupeds must have already reached some tropical region in that undiscovered country where he trumpets and tramps through broad and fertile savannas without fear of pitfalls and other snares for his capture and enslavement.

Almost simultaneously with the death of Chief, was the assassination of Sitting Bull, the Sioux warrior. Was this redskin savage less a hero than the British

Caractacus or the German Orgetorix? Was not his patriotism as pure as that of Horatius, who kept the bridge, or Leonidas, who held the pass with his 300 Spartans?

But Sitting Bull has departed under the constraint of a well aimed pistol shot to the "happy hunting grounds," whither Osceola, Tecumseh, Red Jacket and other Indian braves long ago preceded him. In those virgin forests, untroddenby the foot of the paleface, undisturbed by the ring of the pioneer's ax, he may even now be chasing the bison and the deer, without dread of military molestation. Tell us, if you will, that "the hunter and the deer are both a shade." Far better this delusive dream than the hopelessness of the Atheist's creed.

AT CHRISTMAS TIDE, 1891,

In my boyhood, I contributed occasional verses to the Georgia press. My old-time friends, W. T. Thompson and C. R. Hanleiter, detected a bud of promise in these juvenile effusions. For their kindly recognition I was then and am still profoundly grateful.

At a later period, when a young lawyer, I was struck with the saying of Sir William Blackstone, that the law was a "jealous mistress." Realizing that I had no special skill "to build the lofty rhyme," like the great commentator, I, too, wrote "A Farewell to the Muse." From that date, nearly fifty years ago, I did not attempt poetry. During the recent holidays, however,

I felt afresh my boyish impulse. Weather-bound, and almost bed-ridden, I scribbled on scraps of paper the following lines, which have much of the sadness and but little of the sweetness of the fabled song of the "Dying Swan:"

In My Sixty-sixth Year.

"To-day shalt thou be with Me in Paradise." Words spoken on the cross.

> Lord! I am weary with the stress
>   Of three-score years and more,
> Whose blinding storms and beating waves
>   Have left me stranded on the shore.
>
> Across the stretch of years already trod
>   Ofttimes I've felt the pressure of Thy hand,
> Nor will I doubt, in darkest mood,
>   Thou yet wil't bring me to the better land.
>
> Along that lonely pilgrim way there lie
>   The wrecks of blighted hopes and vanished joys,
> O'er these I breathe an unregretful sigh—
>   These meaner things that chance or change destroys.
>
> But life has loftier aims than these beside,
>   Like far-off stars that neither wax nor wane
> With rolling years, but evermore abide,
>   As magian fires in some high Persian fane.
>
> Wherefore, Oh Christ, I kiss the rod
>   Which smites me downward to the dust;
> Such strokes shall lure me closer to my God,
>   And bind me stronger to my steadfast trust.
>
> Beyond the utmost sweep of life's tempestuous main
>   He hath prepared a restful place for me,
> Where severed friends shall meet again
>   In joyaunce and in harmony.
>
> O'er that sun-bright Beulah lea
>   No darkening storm will ever rise;
> For aye and aye I shall with Thee
>   Be safe at home in Paradise.

www.ingramcontent.com/pod-product-compliance
Lightning Source LLC
Chambersburg PA
CBHW021819230426
43669CB00008B/797